The Revolution

To the Father, whose love is unfailing, the Son, who is worthy of all praise, and the Holy Spirit, whose presence is life and breath. Every good and perfect gift is from You.

God, may You get what You are due: a revolution that returns to its roots, yielding a Bride that returns to her first love.

Table of Contents

Table of Contents

Preface

Thousands of years ago, God spoke about a problem. His people were investing more in their own homes than His in their midst:

Then the word of the Lord came by Haggai the prophet, saying, "Is it time for you yourselves to dwell in your paneled houses while this house *lies* desolate?" Now therefore, thus says the Lord of hosts, "Consider your ways! You have sown much, but harvest little; *you* eat, but *there is* not *enough* to be satisfied; *you* drink, but *there is* not *enough* to become drunk; *you* put on clothing, but no one is warm *enough*; and he who earns, earns wages *to put* into a purse with holes."

Thus says the Lord of hosts, "Consider your ways! Go up to the mountains, bring wood and rebuild the temple, that I may be pleased with it and be glorified," says the Lord. "*You* look for much, but behold, *it comes* to little; when you bring *it* home, I blow *it* away. Why?" declares the Lord of hosts, "Because of My house which *lies* desolate, while each of you runs to his own house" (*New American Standard Bible*, Haggai 1:3-9).

This book is born out of the conviction that this word is as timely today as it was then. We live in a day where the house of God has been neglected, so neglected, it's not even fathomable that someone would invest more time, energy, and resources in building His house than their own! But worse, His house has been so neglected that His people don't even know what it is anymore. Just recently a lifelong church-going believer exclaimed, "We don't have a temple or tabernacle anymore, because Jesus died for us." How many similarly now hear a reference to God's house and His passion for it and say, "But, that is the Old Testament."

Does God care less about His house in our day—that of the New Testament—than He did about the house that bore His name before? We know better, and we see it when we read Jesus' evaluation of His own churches in the book of Revelation. Believer, God has always cared about His habitation, His house. He still does. So, the question for us becomes, "If God were to write a letter to the churches of today, or the American Church at large, what would He say?" Would He commend us? Perhaps! After all, we have the coolest, most hip pastors that Christendom has ever seen. The teachers of today are some of the most entertaining and captivating communicators in all of Christian history. Our musical excellence, million-dollar sound systems, and intricate lighting displays certainly dwarf anything of the past. We are diligent in our stewardship with our finely-tuned strategic plans and execution accountability.

But all of this still begs the question–what is the state of the house of the Lord today? Is God pleased with the current reality? Has anyone asked, and do we need to? After all, if it's "working"—and by working, we mean a lot of people showing up—isn't that an adequate answer? Doesn't attendance speak for itself as to whether God is in a church and good with it? For years, we've assumed the answer is, "Yes," but what if it's not?

On November 4, 2018, the Lord burdened me (Shane) the night before preaching to the point I could not stop weeping over the state of God's house, His Church. I was undone by the emotion His Spirit pressed into and through my soul in the place of groaning and prayer. He laid a word on my heart at that time, based on Isaiah 40, to prepare the way of the Lord, calling for repentance.

As I got up to preach that weekend, I could not preach the transcript I had prepared earlier in the week. Instead, I opened my mouth, and He filled it with a prophetic and fiery rebuke of the state of the Church and the state of our church. As I preached it, I knew a warning from God was flowing through my mouth, and I did not want to get in the way of it. At the same time, I also knew it would be the least-liked sermon that I had ever given. I knew it was the kind of sermon that shrinks crowds in half. I knew it was the kind of preaching that could not sustain the paying of our bills. Some of what you will read in this book was preached on that day.

By the grace of God, I did not edit or soften any part of the message, and when I went back to my seat after preaching, something profound happened. I had what those who are raised in a Southern Baptist background (which I was) and what those who are preaching in a

Presbyterian church (which I was) are not supposed to have—a vision. (Visions had not only been uncommon for me, but I am also a completely conceptual thinker who is incapable of imagining even the simplest picture in my mind and seeing anything. But this, I could see.) I saw Jesus seated on His throne. He stood up. He clapped, and He began to look left and right as if leading others in a collective clap. I understood in my spirit that He was leading Heaven in clapping for what had just taken place on earth. I then knew what Heaven applauds is what the American Church of today condemns, and what the American Church of today applauds is what Heaven condemns.

We have come to the conviction that the American Church has walked our way into a problem so pervasive that we cannot even see it. We assume what is dead is alive. We consider what is bad as good. We deem what is displeasing to the Lord as pleasing.

We need a revolution.

When it comes to much of the American Church, the Church that Jesus purchased with His blood has been taken captive by Babylon. She has been lured into false security and complacency—so seduced by Babylon's prize that she has lost her sight, so enslaved to Babylon's methodologies and philosophies that she cannot recognize she is in chains that bind, and so drunk on Babylon's wine that she no longer knows what it means to be filled with the Spirit.

In many cases, God's platform has been repurposed as a pedestal of ego, with the proclamation of a popular but unauthorized message: "Peace! Peace!" when there is no peace. In far too many instances, we have chased celebrity and despised humility. We have substituted structures for substance. We have pursued polish and programs instead of presence. We have swapped the Spirit for skills and schemes. We have switched to strategy in place of power and to smarts in place of submission.

We need a revolution.

The revolution we hear the Spirit calling for is detailed in this book, but we feel compelled to give a warning at this point. There are some things that once seen, you cannot unsee, and there are some things that once heard, you cannot unhear. If you desire entertainment or simply have curiosity and like to contemplate interesting thoughts, we advise you to put this book down. If you, however, have had a nagging sense deep down that your reading of the New Testament and your experience of living it out in your own church and life have produced a cognitive dissonance that no one's explanations have yet resolved or satisfied, this book may change your life forever. In fact, may so many lives be changed that the world is changed as the revolution is realized. This is our prayer.

Part I

The Revolution Defined

1

Revolution: What Is It?

On Sunday, July 23, 2023, we began to hear from the Lord about the problem in the American Church and the revolution He is calling for. This book is our best attempt to faithfully herald what was heard.

In prayer, we have continued to hear the Lord say that beyond a revival is a reformation, beyond a reformation is a revolution, and that we need a revolution. A revolution can be defined as either: 1) a radical and complete change or 2) a progressive motion of a body around an axis. So, which definition of revolution—and what kind of revolution—does God have in mind?

A good Biblical example of revolution would be the ministry of John the Baptist. By the time John came on the scene, there had been hundreds of years of God's silence. Yes, there had been some triumphs during that time; however, by and large, a people with a history of miracles and mighty acts of God, a people with a history of bonafide prophets releasing the message of God to each generation, now had 400 years of silence.

Then, God broke the silence. What did He say? What did He do? He raised up John the Baptist to lead a revolution—not an activity of incremental improvements in the existing institution, but an overhaul of it. Speaking of what God would accomplish through John, the angel who announced John's birth said,

> "For he will be great in the sight of the Lord; and he will drink no wine or liquor, and he will be filled with the Holy Spirit while yet in his mother's womb. And he will turn many of the sons of Israel back to the Lord their God. It is he who will go *as a forerunner* before Him in the spirit and power of Elijah, TO TURN THE HEARTS OF THE FATHERS BACK TO THE CHILDREN, and the disobedient to the attitude of the righteous, so as to make ready a people prepared for the Lord" (Luke 1:15–17).

Now, if you were present and heard God say that, what would you expect to be true of John? Would you expect him to serve as the lead priest or perhaps as the most popular rabbi in the city? There would be plenty of reasons to imagine those kinds of things.

But look at what we read about John in Luke 1:80: "And the child continued to grow and to become strong in spirit, and he lived in the deserts until the day of his public appearance to Israel." Clearly, God was operating outside of the norms and institutions. He wasn't blessing one of the particular schools or working through the existing programs and paradigms; instead, He was raising up one in the wilderness for this purpose.

Furthermore, notice that God didn't send John out there at the start of his ministry. Scripture is very clear that John lived there *until* he appeared publicly to Israel.

So, we have to ask, "Why would God choose this for John? Why would God want John to be raised in a solitary and desolate wilderness place? Why would God have John go to the same kind of place that the Spirit led Jesus before Jesus began His ministry?" Because it's in the wilderness that an understanding of the revolution is conceived, apart from the mainstream and apart from dependence on the fruits of status quo. It is in the wilderness that one can hear from God clearly both about the problem and the solution.

Now, none of what God was doing with John would have been comfortable or convenient. After all, don't forget who John's dad, Zecharias, was. He was a priest who served in the temple and was part of the institution. Yet, he raised John in the wilderness. So, what do you imagine the other priests were thinking about that? After all, the revelation that God gave Zecharias while he was serving at the altar of incense—and Zecharias being speechless for the next nine months—was well known. You can just imagine the other priests saying, "Really, you are going to raise John as an anointed one who is going to be used by God, and the way you are going to instruct him, the way you are going to teach him, and the way you are going to prepare him to do that is to keep him as far away from us as possible?" That is not exactly the way to win friends and influence people! But, Zecharias wasn't seeking the favor of men. He was seeking God and the favor that comes from God, so he did what God said. He raised John in the wilderness, and the fruit was evidenced.

When John stepped onto the scene, fulfilling the prophetic mandate and calling the people to repentance, there was nothing muddied and nothing murky in his message. He didn't have torn allegiances. He didn't have mixed empathies, and he didn't have divided loyalties. He didn't darken God's counsel by contrasting it with what others said. John just said what God said to say. What was that? "'Repent, for the kingdom of heaven is at hand'" (Matthew 3:2). And to the religious leaders, what did he say? He said to them:

"You brood of vipers, who warned you to flee from the wrath to come? Therefore bear fruit in keeping with repentance; and do not suppose that you can say to yourselves, 'We have Abraham for our father'; for I say to you that from these stones God is able to raise up children to Abraham. The axe is already laid at the root of the trees; therefore every tree that does not bear good fruit is cut down and thrown into the fire.

"As for me, I baptize you with water for repentance, but He who is coming after me is mightier than I, and I am not fit to remove His sandals; He will baptize you with the Holy Spirit and fire. His winnowing fork is in His hand, and He will thoroughly clear His threshing floor; and He will gather His wheat into the barn, but He will burn up the chaff with unquenchable fire" (Matthew 3:7–12).

After 400 years, God finally spoke, and it wasn't only a rebuke and a call to repentance but a dire warning—a warning that God could raise up children of Abraham from others! Had anyone caught wind of what John was going to say ahead of time, none of them would have predicted it was going to go well. Yet, that was the message God had John preach.

Don't miss the radical nature of the whole baptism thing either. John called for Jewish believers to be baptized—not merely for ceremonial uncleanness, but due to the uncleanness of sin itself. At a minimum, this was a strong statement that those who considered themselves clean were unclean. John's immersing outside of the temple was anti-establishment, and the same was true of John being on the other side of the Jordan. In short, John baptizing Jews was a sign to them that they too were on the outside and needed to be brought in.

John was a voice of revolution, a voice of God's revolution, and like any revolution, this revolution had two elements: the problem and the hope of its solution. With any revolution, before the problem is crystallized in both understanding and articulation, there can be a lot of things brewing. There can be widespread discontentment, unhappiness, unsettledness, unease, and even awareness that things are off and wrong; however, there won't be a revolution, because a revolution requires direction. Direction only comes once two truths are brought together: an articulation of the problem and a clarification of the solution. It is then—at that very moment—that a match of hope drops onto the kindling of discontentment and the fires of revolution flare as people realize, "It doesn't have to be this way!" Then, as they change, things change, and the world changes. If you have a problem without hope, you've just got depression. And if you have hope without a problem, you've just got philosophizing and ideating. But a problem and a solution brought together, that is the spark and start of a revolution.

So, what is the Church's problem? And what is its solution?

2

The Problem as It Has Been Defined

In the revolution God started through John the Baptist, the short message God gave him could really be summarized as follows, "That's not the real problem! This is the real problem! You've been defining the problem as Rome, but the real problem is us, right here, overly confident of our covenant status when we don't really love God but live in sin." In short, John redefined the problem.

The revolution needed today must redefine the problem as well. But before we get to that redefinition, let's look at the problem as it's been defined. (Although much in this book can be helpful for churches internationally, when we reference "the Church" from this point forward, we specifically are referring to the American Church unless stated otherwise.) For decades, we have been told that the Church's problem is its declining membership, declining attendance, and declining proportion of and influence over society, and from the moment of diagnosis, there have been many attempts to fix it.

According to Dr. Gary McIntosh, president of the Church Growth Network, "By most accounts the first firmly established church in North America was a Dutch Reformed Church founded in 1628 in New Amsterdam (Manhattan, New York),"[1] and, "[F]rom that day until the early 1960s, most churches and denominations in the United States grew numerically."[2] Then, about 70 years ago, as written in Hoge & Roozen's *Understanding Church Growth and Decline, 1950–1978*, something changed:

An unprecedented period in the life of the North American church began in the mid-1960s. For the first time since records allow us to recall, many major denominations actually stopped growing in membership and began to decline, and the growth rate of most others slowed considerably. This period of decline, which came after nearly two centuries of growth, appears especially stark in comparison with the surge of membership and attendance during the so-called religious revival of the 1950s. The reversal caught many denominational leaders by surprise. Why did the declines occur? . . . by 1973 this question had attracted much attention. Denominational leaders began asking earnest questions[3] (qtd. in McIntosh).

Now, prior to the mid-1960s, can you imagine? The problem for denominations for a couple of hundred years wasn't decline but that such-and-such denomination or church was growing faster! But then, everything changed on a dime. The downward trend started, and the attempts to solve this problem of church decline began quite quickly.

As we dive into the data, it's worth saying as a quick aside, we know there are endless debates about how to rightly define a practicing Christian for the purpose of research and surveys. The attempts to solve the stated problem regarding church attendance and membership have been largely based on those two data points alone, but below that data is something much more sobering. The qualitative gauges underneath the quantitative ones are far worse. The surveys of Americans' faith, leading and lagging indicators alike, show decline from every vantage point possible including attendance,[4] prayer,[5] reading the Bible regularly,[6] membership[7], Biblical worldview[8], and self-profession.[9]

So, what were the attempts to solve the stated problem? Broadly speaking, according to Dr. McIntosh, there have been four major movements in response.[10] I (Shane) was not alive for the first of the four but was deeply involved and immersed in the latter three, both in reading all the books and doing all the things they recommended.

The Church Renewal Movement

The first was the Church Renewal Movement.

Four Movements

According to Dr. McIntosh, this movement "was founded on the premise that if God's people who were already in church, were renewed in their faith, they would naturally reach outward in ministry to those outside the churches."[11] There were two streams, non-charismatic and charismatic, within this movement. The non-charismatic renewal focused on spiritual practices or other changes, while the charismatic renewal focused on the move of the Spirit within the Church. The charismatic stream of this was, of course, present in the Charismatic Renewal among mainline denominations as well as the more decentralized and independent Jesus Movement. In all cases, the focus was on revitalizing the vitality of the body.

What was the outcome of this movement? While there was a lot of renewal among believers, church attendance, church membership, and the proportion of the church to the population statistics didn't improve. In other words, "the problem" wasn't solved, so others rose up with the hope of another and different solution.

The Church Growth Movement

The second movement to address "the problem" was the modern Church Growth Movement.

Four Movements

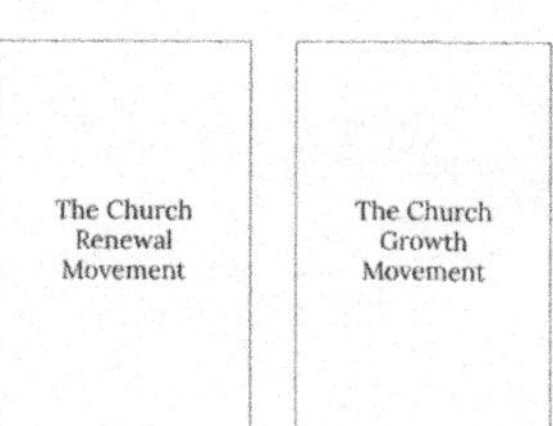

In contrast to the previous movement, the focus of the Church Growth Movement was evangelism. Simply stated, it taught that to reach the lost, you have to focus on them. The Association of Religion Data Archives (ARDA) describes the movement below:

> The Church Growth Movement emerged in the 1970s and 1980s as a network of church consulting firms, conferences, and publications all focused on helping pastors develop strategies to increase the size of their congregations . . . .
>
> Though the network was informal and diffused, the gravity of the movement condensed around certain church growth gurus and pastors like Fuller Theological Seminary professor Donald McGavran, his protege C. Peter Wagner . . . and megachurch pastors Robert Schuller and Bill Hybels.[12]

After its initial start, the movement had several different waves or emphases in the years that followed.

The first wave of the Church Growth Movement to hit America in the 1970s was primarily research focused.[13] (The Church Growth philosophy existed long before this on the *international* scene, as a result of McGavran's philosophy of international missions.) According to the ARDA,

> McGavran's *Understanding Church Growth* (1970) laid the foundation for the Church Growth Movement by encouraging churches to ask themselves four questions: What are the causes of church growth? What are the barriers to church growth?

What are the factors that can make Christian faith a movement among populations? And what principles of church growth are reproducible?[14]

As you can imagine, a seeker-sensitive approach to ministry started here, as for all intents and purposes, people were asking, "What would make people come? What would make people stay?"

As those outside the walls became the target audience, or the customers so to speak, it was an easy jump to move from, "We're called to serve," to a customer service mentality. Will Mancini and Cory Hartman speak to the essence of the seeker church well in their book *Future Church*, recognizing this new shift, which oriented the entirety of the church toward those who did not come to church.[15]

As part of this movement, there was a willingness to separate method from message in order to do what works. To quote Wagner:

Church growth leaders . . . are pragmatic . . . .
If methods currently being used for some evangelistic effort, for example, are not accomplishing the stated goals, they must be revised or scrapped. A strategy must be substituted that will produce the results that God desires.[16]

Along these lines, many shifts took place within the movement that essentially took growth tools from the world of business—such as strategic planning, management, and leadership skills—and applied them to the Church.

Finally, there was a "Church Health Paradigm" within the Church Growth Movement, and, according to McIntosh, its key proponents and their works "simply restated church growth principles wrapped in a church health package."[17] This last adaptation typified, if not originated, the mentality that "healthy things grow"—meaning that if we focus on health and help people get healthy, the church will grow numerically.

So what changes did the Church Growth Movement ultimately call for in the Church? Among many things, it included an emphasis on focusing on the hour on Sunday, highly skilled communication, excellence and relevance in both music and the message, and minimization or elimination of barriers everywhere possible.

As those who both spent most of their ministry life deeply immersed in this particular stream of thought, we can share the formula that produces success as defined by the Church Growth Movement—meaning, growing the church's weekend attendance—is the following:

Excellence + Relevance – Cost = Greatest Attendance

This secret to "success" baffled even church growth experts over the decades, because large-church leaders would often point to some particular program or reason for their growth that when implemented elsewhere was not producing the same results. It's because it wasn't about a particular program. It was whether the hour on Sunday had excellence and relevance at a low cost. (The "cost" of going to any particular church is multi-faceted. Cost can be time, requirements, discomfort, dignity, money, expectations, or any number of things as a result of attending the church itself or the cost of adhering to the teachings of the church.)

This formula works the same in any customer service industry. If you go to a restaurant and the food and environment are good (excellence), it fits your tastes/preferences (relevance), and it's pretty inexpensive (cost), then you will keep going back there. If your tastes/preferences are pretty mainstream, then certainly that restaurant will be one of the most crowded restaurants. While we know that this formula was not articulated and understood as such, what the movement did recognize was that some combination of excellence, relevance, and seeker sensitivity (which lowered cost) worked.

So, did this movement solve the problem? It depends on who you ask and where you look, meaning it had mixed results. When it was executed according to these key ingredients, it often led to more megachurches. The ARDA records, "With the help of Church Growth Movement policies, the 50 megachurches present in 1970 would balloon to 310 by 1990 and 1,250 by 2007."[18] That trend continued in the decades to follow. As of 2022, there were fourteen churches with 20,000 or more reported weekly attendance in the United States,[19] and the vast majority, if not all of them, arose from this movement.

However, this approach did not work for most, for reasons we'll get into later. Overall, the national statistics of church attendance and membership continued to decline, leading people to ask, "Is there a better solution?"

The Emerging/Emergent Movement

The third movement was another attempt to solve the continuing problem by etch-a-sketching the whole thing to find a path that would be more palatable and relatable to society known as the Emerging/Emergent Movement.[20]

Four Movements

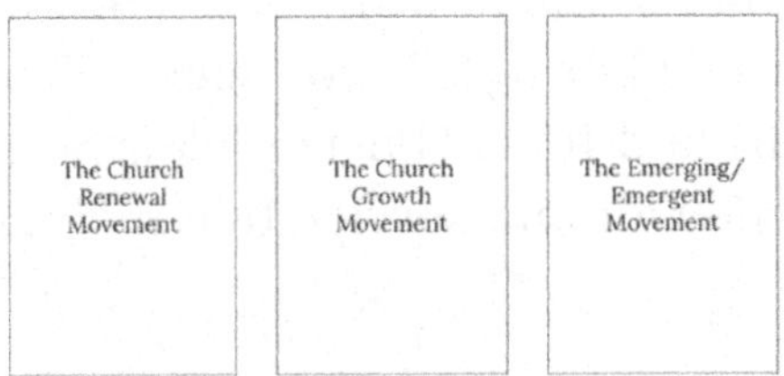

While I (Shane) was an intern in Axis (the former 18–20-something ministry of Willow Creek Community Church), I and many of the other interns dove deeply into the emergent movement and conversation. (Some officially refer to it as a movement, but others classify it as a conversation.) We consumed and did all the things that were trademarks of that movement. (We read the Dan Kimball books, lapped up the McLaren trilogy, personally visited Doug Pagitt's church, and switched our printed ministry fonts to papyrus, all while loading up on candles, incense, crosses, and other tactile experiences for our gatherings.)

What was this movement? Well, it kind of struggled to take on as clear of an identity as the other movements, because it was based on deconstructing the existing models and systems rather than a clearly agreed-upon idea of what it was trying to construct. Sometimes the deconstruction took on a more theological nature, as it did with Brian McLaren who wrote, *A Generous Orthodoxy*. This theological part of the movement led to universalism (i.e., the belief that everyone goes to Heaven) in many cases. Other times, this movement focused less on the message and more on the methods of the church, as was the case with Dan Kimball. In his book, *The Emerging Church: Vintage Christianity for New Generations*, Kimball differentiated between "Seeker-Sensitive As a Lifestyle" and "Seeker-Sensitive As a Style."[21] He argued for a "Post-Seeker Sensitive" style of ministry and worship service that included the following:

> Going back to a raw form of vintage Christianity, which unapologetically focuses on kingdom living by disciples of Jesus. A post-seeker-sensitive worship gathering promotes, rather than hides, full displays of spirituality (extended worship, religious symbols, liturgy, extensive prayer times, extensive use of Scripture and readings, etc.) so that people can experience and be transformed by the message of Jesus.[22]

With the method-altering approach (as opposed to the message-altering approach), older forms of church were ushered in again. Basically, the Church Growth Movement had de-emphasized anything religious, odd, weird, and not relatable to the world so much so that when crosses, incense, candles, liturgy, and churchy-looking stuff came back onto the scene, it seemed really cool for a while—like, the world is changing so much and people wanted to feel something ancient, historic, and rooted.

As you can see, the Emergent Movement was all over the place. However, while traces of it have been incorporated into many churches, it did not solve the stated problem even where the message, the methods, or both were altered.

The Missional Church Movement

The next movement that attempted to solve the problem was the Missional Church Movement.[23]

Four Movements

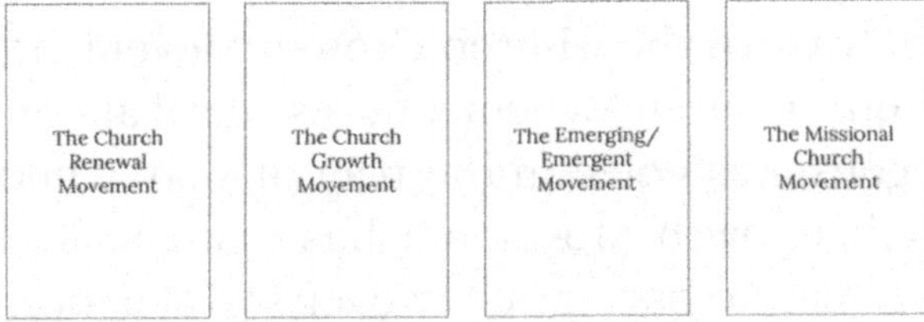

This movement focused on getting outside the walls of the church. The ARDA describes it here:

The missional church movement arose in 1998 when a group of six Protestant theologians published a book entitled *Missional Church: A Vision for the Sending of the Church in North America.* Responding to church decline, as well as "church growth" strategies aimed at attracting non-members into the church, the writers of the *Missional Church* proposed for all members to go out into the world and reflect the gospel in their surrounding communities. According to the writers, missions is at the core of the Christian gospel and requires active engagement with secular society.[24]

As with the previous movements, there were nuances within this movement. In conservative churches, the Missional Church Movement took on a more evangelistic approach (such as missional communities), and in more liberal churches, it took on a more social-justice orientation, such as caring for the poor and marginalized. This movement was similar to the Church Growth Movement in its external focus. However, as McIntosh explains, there was a key difference between them:

> In contrast to the Church Growth Movement, the Missional Church Movement sees social action and evangelism as equal in the plan of God, while the Church Growth Movement has historically held evangelism to have priority over social action in a local congregation.[25]

As one would expect, this difference in perspective led to differences in focus and priority, yet the overall emphasis was to move outside the walls of the Church.

In my (Shane's) later years at Axis, we made this strong switch from emergent to missional, founding missional communities in various apartment complexes. The focus on gathering was greatly reduced, a major separation from the modern Church Growth Movement, in order to "scatter." With a hub of missionally-minded people living in proximity to each other, we threw various parties, get-togethers, grill-outs, and events to reach our neighbors.

Particularly for persons in ministry, this access to the world outside of the church felt like a refreshing alternative, and while celebrated salvations did occur, it did not lead to filling seats on Sunday. The bottom line is that the model did not pay the bills and did not go far as a result. In truth, it also wasn't as replicable as we hoped, as it needed leadership and evangelism giftings present to thrive—two gifts that are found in smaller proportions within Christian communities than the size of missional communities themselves.

As you look at the four movements, you can see how each tended to counterbalance the one before it, with emphasis alternating between internal and external focus. So, which of the movements stuck? The stickiness of any of the attempts and the leaders from the movements all emerged based on one thing—size. Since the problem was defined as "numbers," whichever church grew the most had the loudest voice. Neither the Emergent Movement nor the Missional Church Movement produced many large churches (or any), and so, in some ways, the Church Growth Movement remains the dominant model.

Within this movement, there has been a lot of turnover in the leading voices over the years for a number of reasons. For some, there has been a theological fall as some leaders from this movement, in their attempt to remove every barrier possible to Christianity, eventually began removing any teaching of Scripture they saw as a barrier. For others, there has been a litany of character failures that have resulted in leadership transition.

The current voices of this approach today, which would be those leading some of the largest and most well-known churches now, are doing the same things as their predecessors all these decades later. Yet, what is interesting is that they don't have the level of influence on pastors that the former leaders of this movement used to have, because they aren't saying anything new.

Today, there is a growing disillusionment among many pastors because, despite all the strategies, the data that comes out year after year is worse than the year before on a national level. In addition, many of the pastors went to all those conferences decades ago, tried, and could not get the model to work—not for them. For some, if we're honest, the hill was too steep to simply lead their church through that much change to become relevant, especially with music. For almost all, they were incapable of preaching at the level of "excellence" to effectively execute the model.

So, yes, the Church Growth Movement did and does work for some—still, mainly only in the South of the United States,[26] but not entirely. And almost always, you'll find these pillars of "success" in well-to-do areas where they can afford the infrastructure, bells, and whistles. Why? Because you can't hit the excellence standard without the facilities in part, but also, you can't afford the people who are talented enough to run the model without such resources either.

In addition, those who don't take the bait to do the formula (excellence + relevance – cost = greatest attendance) feel increasingly frustrated, because now every church has another church down the road handing out cotton candy every Sunday. Simply stated, they can't compete when someone else is doing something of such high quality at such a low cost—meaning, the cost of being a Christian.

Should we be surprised by this? Very practically, imagine two churches in the same city. One has great music as well as a very talented and motivational preacher. The other has decent music and a moderately skilled preacher. The preaching at the first church provides people with principles, which they can apply as they see fit, leaves them feeling good about themselves, and tells them all they have to do is believe in Jesus and look to Him for self-help and self-improvement. The teaching at the second church calls people to obey Christ's commands in all things, including relationships, priorities, and finances. What do we expect to happen? We expect to see exactly what we see happen—the first draws far more people, while the second draws fewer people due to it being viewed as too costly and too extreme.

This isn't just an illustration. It is reality. Statistically, there is an inverse relationship between a church's size and its pastors having a Biblical worldview. Research done by the Cultural Research Center at Arizona Christian University (published in May 2022) found the following:[27]

Average Adult Attendance	Percent [of Pastors] with Biblical Worldview
250 or less adults	42%
251 or more adults	15%

Clearly, having a Biblical worldview has a very strong and inverse relationship with attendance; however, it is not just with pastors, as people are voting with their feet as to what they want. Otherwise stated, people prefer to be where pastors have a low Biblical worldview.

So, what was the net effect of each and all of these movements? The following graph of "American Religiosity,"[28] which evaluates several elements including attendance at services to assess religious activity, answers the question.

"The Great Decline: 60 Years of Religion in America"

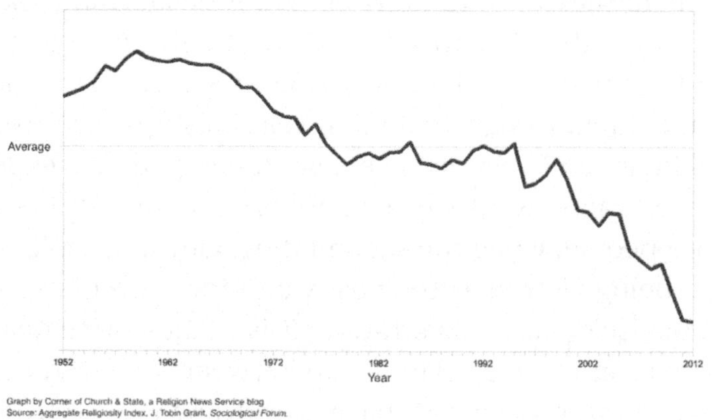

Graph by Corner of Church & State, a Religion News Service blog
Source: Aggregate Religiosity Index, J. Tobin Grant, *Sociological Forum*.

But it's worse than it looks. This data ends in 2012. What about the data since then? What we have observed in reviewing dozens of studies is that while the drop from the 1960s has been quite steady, the rate of decline from 2010 onwards has increased dramatically.

In 2021, the Pew Research Center released a study with the following findings:

- "Self-identified Christians make up 63% of [the] U.S. population in 2021, down from 75% a decade ago."[29]

This is staggering and eclipses the rate of prior

decline, with a decrease of more than a percent per year!
- Religion is very important for 41% of adults in 2021, compared to 56% in 2007 (15% decline in 14 years).[30]

Where does a decline of one percent a year leave us in the not-too-distant future? Although we are in the early stages of being a post-Christian society now, we are on the path to looking like Europe does today. Below are some facts:
- In 2022, the Pew Research Center found that the percentage of "U.S. adults who say they generally attend religious services once a month or more has dropped slightly, from 33% in 2019 to 30% in 2022."[31]
- Another analysis by the Institute for Family Studies, based on the American Family Survey, found that "religious attendance has declined significantly in the past two years. The share of regular churchgoers is down by 6 percentage points, from 34% in 2019 to 28% in 2021."[32]

In all cases, we're seeing something similar, at or beyond a percent decrease per year since 2010.

A recent Gallup study asked Americans if they happened "to attend church, synagogue, mosque or temple in the last seven days, or not?"[33] (Granted, this data includes a wider pool than just Christians and church attendance; however, given the predominant religion of America is Christianity, we think this data is still helpful.) The most recent findings, compared to historical results, are significant. The period between 1962–1972 saw a six percent decrease, which is of course substantial, but, from 1972 forward, things were relatively static, until the decade from 2012 until 2022. In those ten years, there was a 10% decrease from 40% down to 30%.[34]

We do not know of any existing study that explains this phenomenon. We would, however, offer two personal and prayerful insights—one explaining the attendance dip pre-COVID and the second explaining the attendance dip post-COVID. First, the pre-COVID time of decline coincides with the period we began to hit a tipping point with LGBTQ+ advocacy in society. In short, we entered into the first period in American history where being associated with Christ and the Church costs you more than it benefits you in society.

Second, as it relates to the post-COVID decline, during a crisis, more people typically turn to God, but there is also a historical precedent for that turning to be followed by a leaving after the crisis ends. For example, the first Church decline in the 1960s followed the post-WWII religious surge. When COVID first hit, we also saw an uptick in faith engagement. But, afterward, we saw it plummet. Why? It is in the nature of humanity to turn to God in a crisis when we are afraid. However, it is also in the heart of humanity once we experience reprieve (especially if we believe that reprieve is on account of our own doing, such as developing a vaccine) and feel safe and secure to then turn to God in accusation: "Why did You let this happen?" We believe these human dynamics account for the initial turning toward God at the onset of the pandemic, as well as the post-pandemic decrease in church engagement.

All to say, the rate of decline has increased lately, and the post-COVID reality seems to be an acceleration more than a bounceback. So much effort has gone into solving the problem, and yet the problem has not been solved—only accelerated!

How disillusioned are the pastors of America? According to a 2022 Barna study, pastors surveyed were asked, "Have you given real, serious consideration to quitting being in full-time ministry within the last year?" Among those surveyed, 42% said, "Yes!"[35] Why such a high percentage? No one wants to wake up and feel like a failure, and certainly, no one wants to wake up tomorrow and feel like an even bigger failure than yesterday.

In summary, we have a problem. We now have churches exponentially larger than the largest churches of the 1960s, but the capital "C" American Church is exponentially smaller than the capital "C" American Church of the 1960s. Is that a win? Is it solving the problem really? Obviously not. The problem keeps getting worse. How crazy!

After decades of smart people trying to give the people what they want, and those churches that can deliver it (high quality and high relevance at a low cost) growing like gangbusters, **the bottom line is that we've lost a nation**.

What is being said now to try to fix it? Nothing, honestly—except to perhaps adapt to our times and accept online church as the new reality, which is no change other than lowering the cost even more than we already have. Now you don't even have to get dressed! Other than that, oddly enough, there isn't much being said right now, period. When you read the little that is out there today, it's like people know the problem is huge, but they are suggesting tiny knob turns and slight slider pushes. It's weird.

What does all this boil down to? Basically, the best answer to the stated problem is still the same formula, but no one wants to admit it.

Excellence + Relevance − Cost = Greatest Attendance

This is what it takes to grow the church. There's your golden formula to fill the seats.

But again, what if you are located in one of the poorest of places? How can you afford to bring such excellence? We're not seeing that kind of success there, because the formula doesn't work there. That should concern us gravely if we have eyes to see. Why? Because if it won't work where there aren't the resources for it to work, then what is drawing people? It's not Jesus. It's the resources. If the formula requires substantial resources to get the desired results, it's impoverished.

So, what is the revolution? Is it just to do these things bigger and better than everyone else? That, by the way, has gotten harder and harder, because now everyone can hear the sermons of the most gifted communicators in the world at a fingertip at any moment making the standards of excellence impossibly high. It's not only the skill in delivery, but it's the cool factor—the IT factor, which only some people have, and the impact the message has on the listener (how it makes them feel, meaning really good). As a result, we have an increasing number of people who don't go to church but watch someone out of state online, from their sofa, at the lowest cost imaginable while receiving the highest quality imaginable.

If we have eyes to see, the problem we are facing is the same that movie theaters are experiencing. When attending the gathering is framed up in terms of "what it can do for me," and "I have more comfortable seats at home, a comparable sound system, and don't even have to get myself and my family up and around to drive there," it's a no brainer. "I'll stay home." And, after a while of staying at home and doing that, someone can easily come to think, "What difference will it make if I watch a service, or a portion of it, or just listen to a podcast at some other point in the week?"

In our customer-oriented mentality within our me-oriented society, many have come to view the gathering as increasingly irrelevant and unnecessary. What we scrambled to turn into a front door has become the largest backdoor in the history of the Church. This is where we are. Is there any alternative?

3

Our Solutions' Problems

For decades, we've been told that the problem of the Church is its declining membership, declining attendance, and declining proportion of society. As we saw in the last chapter, numerous solutions have been put forth to solve the decline, but not only have they not solved it, they have actually accelerated it. That's a problem, of course—a massive one. But, is the only issue with these solutions their apparent failure to solve the so-called problem?

The reality is that our "solutions" to solve the stated problem of church growth have actually wreaked havoc on the Church. In other words, our attempts to solve a problem have created greater problems. What are they? How have our attempts impacted the Church in America? Let's think about that a little. If the greatest problem is a size problem, what are you going to do? You are going to do whatever people want and whatever people like—that's what.

After decades of doing this, and all pastors everywhere being evaluated by one thing (church growth), pastors have become, not God's untainted and untethered heralds, but politicians who are voted in or out by feet. Churches have become movie theaters showcasing their features and offering concessions, and the Church has drifted toward a democracy of sorts and away from a Kingdom.

One megachurch leader used to have a sign on his door, "What does the customer want?" What happens to the Word when the Church gives "the customers" what they want? What happens to the Spirit? What happens to worship and prayer? What happens to the Church? We don't have to guess. We just have to glance back in our rearview mirror.

Word

When it comes to the Word, what did people want? People wanted less lengthy messages and wanted them on more comfortable topics, and so that is what, by and large, the Church has provided.

In our own research of the sermons of some of the most popular preachers in America, we found that the words "sin" and "repentance" were strangely missing, largely replaced with an exhortation to "do better" or "get better." We also found the gospel—that Jesus and Jesus alone is Lord and Savior and alone can forgive one of his/her sins and bring him/her into everlasting life—is strangely missing from many of the sermons of the most popular Christian preachers. It seems that our emphatic assertion of our purpose being the Great Commission has been a charade hiding the true and more insidious purpose of the "great attendance."

Studies have discovered that the most distinctive aspects of the evangelical tradition (which is widely regarded as having the highest respect for the inerrancy of Scripture) are quite rare in sermons by those who identify as evangelical. For example, the Pew Research Center analyzed nearly 50,000 sermons from more than 6,000 Christian churches (that tended to have larger than average congregations) in the Spring of 2019. The findings are troubling on multiple fronts:

> [S]ermons from evangelical churches were three times more likely than those from other traditions to include the phrase "eternal hell" (or variations such as "eternity in hell"). However, a congregant who attended every service at a given evangelical church in the dataset had a roughly one-in-ten chance of hearing one of those terms at least once during the study period. By comparison, that same congregant had a 99% chance of hearing the word "love."[1]

The same study found the words "trespass . . . sin" were only found in 9% of evangelical sermons as well[2], which certainly matched our informal personal study.

This Pew Research Center study also revealed that tougher topics, culturally speaking, are rarely addressed. "[J]ust 4% of sermons shared on U.S. church websites in the spring of 2019 discussed abortion even once – and when they did, it was rarely mentioned repeatedly."[3] Additionally and interestingly, the study found that "[c]ongregations with fewer members tend to hear more references to abortion than those with larger memberships."[4]

With the people wanting less confrontation of difficult subjects, many churches also refused to preach on homosexuality or transgenderism. Why? Because it would be too big of a barrier. In many instances, the Church's approach instead has been to just get people in the doors and hope God works that out with them eventually. It's become quite regular to hear pastors who hold to a Biblical, historic, orthodox view of marriage, gender, and sexuality be surprised when they discover their own committed congregants are liking and giving approval online to various pride posts. They are shocked at this outcome, but at the same time, they have avoided teaching what God has revealed in His Word on these topics.

When it comes to any number of difficult and controversial topics, can many pastors today say what Paul said in Acts 20:26-27? "'Therefore, I testify to you this day that I am innocent of the blood of all men. For I did not shrink from declaring to you the whole purpose of God.'" Of course, Paul was referencing Ezekiel, ensuring that all of us preachers, prophets, and teachers would know this truth still stands for us today.

"Son of man, I have appointed you a watchman to the house of Israel; whenever you hear a word from My mouth, warn them from Me. When I say to the wicked, 'You will surely die,' and you do not warn him or speak out to warn the wicked from his wicked way that he may live, that wicked man shall die in his iniquity, but his blood I will require at your hand. Yet if you have warned the wicked and he does not turn from his wickedness or from his wicked way, he shall die in his iniquity; but you have delivered yourself" (Ezekiel 3:17-19).

We think of watchmen in terms of prayer warriors, but the context of Ezekiel was saying what God says to say—without edits or omissions.

Paul, whose goal was to reach Gentiles, did not minimize the differences between walking by the Spirit and living according to the flesh. He wrote to the Ephesians:

> So this I say, and affirm together with the Lord, that you walk no longer just as the Gentiles also walk, in the futility of their mind, being darkened in their understanding, excluded from the life of God because of the ignorance that is in them, because of the hardness of their heart; and they, having become callous, have given themselves over to sensuality for the practice of every kind of impurity with greediness (Ephesians 4:17-19).

So, the apostle to the Gentiles told the Gentiles that they were darkened in their understanding, excluded from life in God, hard of heart, calloused, and indulgent in sensuality and impurity. For Paul, saying that had zero contradiction to his evangelistic gifting, as he understood the gospel was a call to repent from sin and turn toward faith in Jesus. Today's gospel sounds very different, does it not?

Our approach to Christendom in America is largely unrecognizable when we read the New Testament today. But, should we be surprised? A new study (*American Worldview Inventory 2021-2022*) from the Cultural Research Center at Arizona Christian University, where Dr. George Barna serves as the Director of Research, "found that just 37% of Christian pastors in the United States have a biblical worldview."[5] The results are even more concerning when segmented by pastoral role[6]:

- Only 41% of senior/lead pastors possess a Biblical worldview.
- Only 13% of teaching pastors hold a Biblical worldview.
- Only 12% of children's and youth pastors have a Biblical worldview.
- Only 4% of executive pastors hold a Biblical worldview.

As an aside, the positions of teaching pastor and executive pastor are almost exclusive to very large megachurches, whereas the data on lead pastors applies to churches of all sizes.

If the majority of Christian pastors in America do not have a Biblical worldview what do they have?

"[L]ess than 1% of pastors embody a worldview other than Biblical Theism (i.e., the biblical worldview)," researchers said. "Instead, their prevailing worldview is best described as Syncretism, the blending of ideas and applications from a variety of holistic worldviews into a unique but inconsistent combination that represents their personal preferences. More than six out of 10 pastors (62%) have a predominantly syncretistic worldview."[7]

Culture is impacting the Church, including pastors, more than the Church is impacting culture. After reviewing the results of the study, Barna concluded the following, and we agree, "'It certainly seems that if America is going to experience a spiritual revival, that awakening is needed just as desperately in our pulpits as in the pews.'"[8]

In the overwhelming majority of American churches today, the Word of God has been shrunk back from preaching the full counsel of God's Word. Full obedience to all God's commands is not being taught or expected. Christianity is no longer costly, but challenging at most and merely complementary in many cases.

Our concessions have had a cost. The research shows that even church-going Christians are hard to call Christians by any stretch of the imagination. In his book *Revolution*, Barna found that "[o]nly 9 percent of all born-again adults had a biblical worldview,"[9] with a "biblical worldview" being defined as belief in the most fundamental Christian doctrines. Nine percent!

> [This means] that less than one out of every ten Christians age eighteen or older believes that absolute moral truth exists, believes that such truth is contained in the Bible, and possesses a handful of core beliefs that reflect such truth. Those beliefs include a certainty that the Bible is accurate in its teachings; Jesus lived a sinless life on earth; Satan is real, not symbolic; all believers are responsible for sharing their faith in Christ with others; the only means to salvation is through God's grace; and God is the all-knowing and all-powerful creator of the universe who still rules it today.[10]

How can that be? Why is the Church now filled with those who do not believe what Christians believe? It's the result of our incremental discipleship philosophy and teaching. By shrinking back from teaching the full counsel of God's Word to a portion of it, our offerings have created appetites. To quote one pastor friend of ours, Darren Whitehead, "There is milk, and there is meat; then there is shaking the milk and simply serving the froth off the top." We now have theologically malnourished churches filled with those who feel full.

Along these lines, the qualitative data is more concerning than the quantitative. For example, the *American Worldview Inventory 2021–2022* records the following:

- "Belief that the Bible is the accurate and reliable word of God [went] from 70% [of the U.S adult population (age 18 and over)] in 1991 to 41% in 2021."[11]
- "Belief in the existence of God as the all-knowing, all-powerful creator of the universe who still rules the world today [went] from 86% in 1991 to 46% in 2021."[12]

What do these statistics show? Along with others, these statistics point to the decline in the proportion of Americans who can be described as born-again Christians based on their actual beliefs (as opposed to unreliable estimates based on self-identification).

On top of that, the following statistics from the *American Worldview Inventory 2021–22*[13] reveal the substance or lack thereof underneath the profession of many self-identifying Christians in the U.S. adult population, as they hold the following beliefs that are incompatible with historic, orthodox Christianity:

- "66% say that having faith matters more than which faith you adopt."
- "64% say that all religious faiths are of equal value."
- "58% believe that if a person is good enough, or does enough good things, they can earn their way into Heaven."

- "58% contend that the Holy Spirit is not a real, living being but is merely a symbol of God's power, presence or purity."
- "52% claim that determining moral truth is up to each individual; there are no moral absolutes that apply to everyone, all the time."
- "[O]nly one-third (34%) believes that people are born into sin and can only be saved of the consequences by Jesus Christ."

In short, at least 66% of self-professed Christians are thoroughly not Christians, as it's impossible to have faith that Jesus is Lord and Savior, while simultaneously claiming it does not matter whether your faith is in Jesus or another. Likewise, it is impossible to have faith that Jesus is Lord and Savior while not believing that one can only be saved from the consequence of sin by Jesus Christ.

Full surrender was the starting line in the Bible. But, in our attempts to lower the barriers to entry, full surrender has been considered the finish line, and as a result, almost nobody gets there. We have become thoroughly unbiblical in our so-called teaching of the Scriptures. Our teachings send the message, "Work your way toward laying down your life for Jesus and consider dying eventually." Why do we take such liberties to change what Jesus said? He never said that. He said,

"If anyone wishes to come after Me, he must deny himself, and take up his cross and follow Me. For whoever wishes to save his life will lose it; but whoever loses his life for My sake will find it" (Matthew 16:24–25).

Too many pulpits today are occupied by puppets of popularity peddling an unauthorized message that is antithetical to and an assault on the Word of God.

Our so-called solutions to the so-called problem have created more and greater problems. We need a revolution.

Spirit

How have these solutions impacted what happened with the Church and the Spirit? There was a conflation of ideas to reduce the barriers to coming to church and staying. In the wake of modernity, one of these was to stifle the supernatural. The supernatural was out of style and unintellectual—kind of like believing in a good luck charm: "We don't want to look like one of those stupid, superstitious people who believe in miracles!" In the wake of the Enlightenment, the prize of our culture's eyes was to be seen as rational. So, in the attempt to be relevant, Christianity avoided the supernatural, "weird" stuff—not entirely of course, but even among those who were open to the Spirit, many approached it from the belief that it could help solve the growth problem.

As a result, even among those who claim to be born-again Christians, "62% contend that the Holy Spirit is not a real, living being, but is merely a symbol of God's power, presence, or purity."[14] We would certainly expect those identifying as born-again to have a higher percentage of people holding a Biblical view than those only generally identifying as Christian. However, this number is four percent *less* than all self-identified Christians. This tells us that self-identifying as born-again or evangelical no longer yields any substantial meaning or differentiation in the data from generally identifying as Christian.

Major players in the open-to-the-Spirit streams parted ways over whether the Holy Spirit "stuff" should be front room or backroom. (Imagine being the Spirit of God and hearing others talk about You and what You do like that?) Those who thought the things of the Spirit would be a problem for church growth moved the things of the Spirit to the backroom. Those who thought the things of the Spirit would help reach the lost moved them to the front room. The Holy Spirit became a means to the end—not how can we submit to Him, not how can we be led by Him, but how can we use Him to accomplish our ends? If you follow the charismatic stream at large, you'll see that the Holy Spirit has been moved to the back room more and more.

If you define the problem wrong, even if you're on track to the right solution to the *real* problem, you'll abandon the solution. All to say, when it comes to the Spirit, the Church is not filled with the Spirit, but instead, intoxicated with Babylon's wine—the wine of self-sufficiency. Along these lines, the Church Growth Movement has been saying, "We've got to get rid of all the odd stuff, the odd language, the encounters, the in-house speak, and the in-house activity. We need to normalize, to naturalize." That is why there is a front-facing room and a backroom even among those who say, "Yes," to the Holy Spirit, at least in part.

In place of encountering God, churches primarily tried to give people an encounter with His love, reasoning that if people encounter and hear about God's love, it will grow our churches. After all, everyone wants to be where they are loved. True, but not everyone wants a Lord who loves them. It turns out that most of humanity does not want a Lord over their life at all, other than their own unholy trinity of me, myself, and I.

Do you see that God's presence, at large, has come to be viewed as a problem, a barrier? In many ways, the Church can be likened to a man who married up. As he married into his wife's family, much came his way in terms of gains, access, and means, but there was a problem. His wife didn't fit in well with the company that he kept and the guests he was accustomed to bringing into his home. So, when he had company, he said to his wife, "Hey, I love you. I don't want you to go. But, while the company comes, if you could stay in the backroom, I'd appreciate it. You don't mind, do you? I need to ask you not to be seen or heard, because they may not understand you or like you. But, I love you. You know that!"

This is exactly what God has suffered from His Church. What kind of love is that? And yet, it's done in His own house.

Worship

How else have these solutions to the problem impacted Christianity? What happens to worship when the problem is that people don't want to come and the solution is to cater to customers' wants and wishes? Worship becomes ministry not to God, but to people. Barna's research reveals the impact this has had:

> Only one out of every four churched believers says that when they worship God, they expect Him to

be the primary beneficiary of their worship. (Most people say they expect to get the most from the experience.)[15]

Like Saul wanting David to play his harp to ease his demons, so church music has become not about God but about its impact on one's emotional state. Songs have become about what God is going to do for me to the point that you start to wonder who we are worshiping. People walk out saying, "What did you think of the music?" But no one is asking, "What did God think of my worship?" If people dance or lie prostrate in the aisle, they get asked not to do that anymore, because, "We don't want to scare our guests."

The worship of the Church is now that of a nation of priests who have taken after Hophni and Phinehas, those wicked sons of Eli, who poked their forks into the offering and withheld for themselves (1 Samuel 2:12-17). The assembly whose praise is intended to create an environment of Heaven on earth—that the King of glory may dwell in the midst of His people's praises—has instead become a visible testimony to the world that our God isn't that great, doesn't deserve that much praise, and isn't all that loved by His people. We wonder why our methods have not led to the evangelization of a nation that already does not think that God is that good or that great, worthy of all of our love, or worthy of any of our love for that matter, but why would they be moved by such apathy?

In short, the house of worship, intended to be the living embodiment of the call to love the Lord our God with all our heart, soul, mind, and strength, has become a house of idolatrous withholding. Its so-called worship declares, not the greatness of God, but His mediocrity. We need a revolution.

Prayer

And how has our best solution to the so-called problem impacted prayer? Revivals were all birthed in the place of prayer, but where did all the prayer go? Prayer has all but disappeared in the Church. Why? Because no one interpreted the problem's solution as needing God more.

In fact, prayer has often been interpreted as laziness and inactivity. "Don't pray unless you are willing to be a part" is true, but it has been shortened practically and mostly to, "Don't pray. Do it yourself." What does God make of our prayerlessness? What is its root according to Him? "The wicked, in the haughtiness of his countenance, does not seek *Him*" (Psalm 10:4).

Even where there is prayer, it often says, "God, give *me* the strength, the opportunity, the audience, and the hearing." In other words, "God, You give the raw materials, the raw essentials, and I will build it from there." In the world, we mature and graduate into independence. In the Kingdom, however, we mature and graduate into greater dependence.

Major prayer movements are quite rare today and have largely been led in the parachurch sphere. Why? Well, neither prayer nor what God could do are part of the equation of excellence + relevance - cost = greatest attendance. After all, God humbles His vessels—He is not out to make them look excellent. God has antiquated ideas—they are not considered relevant. And the Lord requires dying to yourself every day, so much for low cost!

Our formulas of success have made the house of prayer a house of prayerlessness. We need a revolution.

The Next Generation

With each decade since the 1960s, the generational baton pass of faith has come with more and more drops than the prior. According to the *American Worldview Inventory 2021-22*, the numbers are plummeting at a striking rate:

> [W]hile four out of 10 people 55 or older (40%) can be classified as theologically defined born-again Christians (i.e., categorized as such based on their beliefs about personal salvation), far fewer Gen X adults (26%) fit within the segment, but just one out of every six Millennials (16%) meets the criterion.[16]

Every generation is losing more of the next generation. Does this reality break our hearts as much as it does God's? Do we grieve this reality? Do we pray for the reversal of it? Are we so burdened that we will do anything necessary to see it change?

Jesus told us in Matthew 7:16–20 that we could judge a tree by its fruit. The clear verdict is that the fruit of the Church has become bad. Yet, we keep perpetuating the same tree. If a son of hell is one who is not saved from the consequence of his/her sin by faith in Jesus Christ alone, then the data seems to suggest we have become those Jesus spoke of in Matthew 23:15: "'[Y]ou travel around on sea and land to make one proselyte; and when he becomes one, you make him twice as much a son of hell as yourselves.'"

With every attempt to fix the stated problem, more and more of each generation have fallen out of the flock. We need a revolution.

4

The Real Problem

As we have seen, none of the proposed solutions have solved the problem of the numeric decline of the Church. However, all of them have had very heavy side effects on the Church, to the point that if we read the New Testament before we experienced the Church, we'd find ourselves saying in most cases, "How did it get from that (what we are reading) to this (what we are experiencing)?"

For years, instead of God being the center of the Church regardless of cost, leaders of the Church have dismissed anything of God (whether God's activity, God's praise, God's words, God's Word, or even God Himself) that got in the way of solving the growth problem and believed they were justified in doing so. But, in how many churches has God looked and seen—and does God look and see—that what is ultimately worshiped, bowed down to, submitted to, feared, and loved is a room full of people even if He isn't there?

If you went to doctors for 60 years and none of the solutions for your diagnosis worked, somewhere along the way, you would start to question if the diagnosis was correct, wouldn't you? However, when it comes to the Church, no one has questioned if the problem we're trying to solve is the right one. So, let's ask that now. When God looks at the Church, what does He see? What is His diagnosis and chief concern? Is it "too few people" that tops His list?

There is no doubt about what is in the heart of God for those who are far from Him. We see God's love for and pursuit of the lost throughout Scripture, and Jesus' commands to His disciples echo this. In Matthew 28:18–20, we read,

> And Jesus came up and spoke to them, saying, "All authority has been given to Me in heaven and on earth. Go therefore and make disciples of all the nations, baptizing them in the name of the Father and the Son and the Holy Spirit, teaching them to observe all that I commanded you; and lo, I am with you always, even to the end of the age."

Likewise, we read in Acts 1:8,

> "[Y]ou will receive power when the Holy Spirit has come upon you; and you shall be My witnesses both in Jerusalem, and in all Judea and Samaria, and even to the remotest part of the earth."

God loves the world and longs for all who do not know Him to be saved (1 Timothy 2:3-4). It's clear God sees people perishing as a problem, and a very significant one! But is that the Church's greatest problem? And, what if our attempts to answer the wrong problem have made the real problem worse? What if we need a revolution to address the real problem?

So, let's consider this. When we observe God throughout history as revealed in His Word, do we see Him say, "My chief concern is how many"? It is a major concern. It's not a minor one. It is a major theme. It's not a subtheme. But what does God spend most of His time addressing? What does He spend most of His time doing? Is it getting more or is it getting hearts? We tend to equate the two, but when we look at what God says and does, we see they are not one and the same.

In the Old Testament, after God saves the entire nation of Israel for Himself, what does He address most often? Does He express joy that He has the numbers (of a whole nation) and emphasize the desire to get more just like them? Or, does God spend the majority of His time addressing the hard-hearted, dying, and even dead state of His peoples' hearts? Numbers and hearts are not one and the same. God is after whole hearts. He spoke about this in Isaiah, and Jesus repeated it in Matthew 15:7–8: "You hypocrites, rightly did Isaiah prophesy of you: 'THIS PEOPLE HONORS ME WITH THEIR LIPS, / BUT THEIR HEART IS FAR AWAY FROM ME.'" If it was true of the Old Testament worshippers and true of those first-century worshippers, can we assume it's not true of our churches today? We should not and cannot.

Additionally, if numbers are God's greatest concern, it's really hard to make sense of Jesus, isn't it? After all, what did Jesus do? Did He make concessions to cut out cost? Did He say, "I'll take whatever I can get. I'm just happy with one step today!" At the individual level, think of the rich young man (Matthew 19:16–22). He wanted to follow Jesus, but Jesus didn't just say, "Yes!" Instead, Jesus, knowing there was one thing this man would not be willing to do, made the full surrender requirements of discipleship clear—requirements the man was unwilling to meet, and the man went away sad. So much for hiding the barrier of the cost and going after an incremental following of Jesus, right?

Now some will read this and say, "But I thought Jesus was—and is—love?" He is. In fact, that very text says, "Jesus felt a love for him and said to him, 'One thing you lack . . .'" (Mark 10:21). It turns out true love and our definition of love today are not the same. If reaching more people is the greatest problem, the chief problem, what do we make of what Jesus did? Did He just check out, lose His mind momentarily, and get that interaction wrong?

What about the other interactions Jesus had? When one man wanted to go bury his father before following Jesus, what did Jesus say? "Of course. I understand. Do that and catch up with us when you're done." No, He said, "'Allow the dead to bury their own dead'" (Luke 9:60). From just these two instances, you almost get the sense that Jesus did not see numbers as the greatest problem!

Let's talk about Jesus' famous teaching in John 6. Things are going well. Ministry is growing. If there was ever a time that you would have just ridden the momentum that would have been it. Give the people a spur-you-on message. Give them a reason to keep coming. Say enough to get them to move toward a step of growth, but don't say anything, of course, that would be a stumbling block. Stumbling blocks and masses don't go together after all.

What does Jesus do? Facing one of the greatest crowds He had up to that point, having an opportunity to reach masses and have them added to His numbers, He preached one of the hardest messages to hear, and how did people respond? We are told in John 6:66, "As a result of this many of His disciples withdrew and were not walking with Him anymore." They literally chose an eternity apart from Him at that moment, but Jesus would not compromise in the slightest! Then, He turned to the 12, not the 200, the 12, and said, "'You do not want to go away also, do you?'" (John 6:67). You talk about burning it down to a remnant, and Jesus was willing! Why?

Did Jesus believe the greatest problem was a numbers problem? Clearly not. If He did, there is no rhyme or reason to His activity. Jesus knew there was a greater problem, a real problem. What was that problem? When His disciples called Him out on the difficulty of His teaching, how did He respond?

> But Jesus, conscious that His disciples grumbled at this, said to them, "Does this cause you to stumble? *What* then if you see the Son of Man ascending to where He was before? It is the Spirit who gives life; the flesh profits nothing; the words that I have spoken to you are spirit and are life. But there are some of you who do not believe" (John 6:61–64).

So, after nearly everyone leaves, Jesus is still concerned about the one who is there but not really there. Jesus wasn't after bodies that had cavities for hearts. He was after a true following, where every heart was His.

We are surprised by that, but we really shouldn't be when we consider the whole of Scripture. After all, when God spoke to the nation of Israel, what did He say and require of them? "'You shall love the Lord your God with all your heart and with all your soul and with all your might'" (Deuteronomy 6:5). Likewise, when Jesus was asked what the greatest commandment was, what did He say? "'YOU SHALL LOVE THE LORD YOUR GOD WITH ALL YOUR HEART, AND WITH ALL YOUR SOUL, AND WITH ALL YOUR MIND.' This is the great and foremost commandment" (Matthew 22:37–38).

When we look at Jesus speaking to the church of Ephesus, what does He say? "'But I have *this* against you, that you have left your first love'" (Revelation 2:4). Now, hearing Jesus say that, we expect this church to be a total mess—like there could not possibly be one thing that they are getting right. But is that the case? No, it is not. Look at what Jesus says just before this:

> 'I know your deeds and your toil and perseverance, and that you cannot tolerate evil men, and you put to the test those who call themselves apostles, and they are not, and you found them *to be* false; and you have perseverance and have endured for My name's sake, and have not grown weary. But I have *this* against you, that you have left your first love' (Revelation 2:2–4).

Whoa! Good deeds? They had those! Hard toil? Check. Perseverance? Check. Testing and discerning? Check. Endurance for His name's sake? Check. They had a lot of good going on! From that list, you would gather they are a very strong Bible church, but what does Jesus say? "You have left your first love." They had so many right actions but lacked the first love.

Does Jesus consider that a small infraction? No! He goes on to say what the consequence of that is: "'I am coming to you and will *remove your lampstand* out of its place—unless you repent'" (Revelation 2:5, emphasis added). That sounds serious, doesn't it? What is the lampstand? The very last verse of the prior chapter tells us, "'[T]he seven lamp-stands are the seven churches'" (Revelation 1:20). So, to paraphrase, Jesus says, "I am going to remove your church, your ekklésia" (the Greek word for a "called assembly").

How does that work? Couldn't they still gather without His lampstand, and wouldn't that constitute a church? After all, they would be singing psalms to the Father, hymns to Jesus, and Spirit songs as well. They would be reading the Scriptures and all that. How could that not be church? Because the church is a gathering where the One who called the gathering is present. If Jesus is not there, it's not a church, not a lampstand anymore. The lampstand represents His presence. Jesus was essentially saying, "I will remove My presence. You might think you're gathered in My name, but you're not. And, My presence has been removed."

Think about that—a church can be a church in name only. We have a nation of churches for whom many have had their lampstand removed. For some, this took place decades ago, and for others, it was just days ago. Yet, no one has even noticed. His gathering has become so devoid of His presence, so not about His presence, the threat of losing it or the reality of losing it would be insignificant to most.

We need to remember what the gathering is intended to be as God defines it—it is intended to be the tabernacle of the New Testament, the place where God dwells in the midst of His people. When people come into the gathering, the undeniable exclamation and praise should be, "Surely God is in this place, in our midst."

What God has desired, what He has set out to get, has never changed from the beginning, and it doesn't change at the end. His design and desire are not distance but to be in the midst of His people. Isn't this what we see in Eden? Aren't we told that God walked among Adam and Eve in the garden (Genesis 3:8)?

Isn't God in the midst of His people what we read about in the new Heaven?

> And I heard a loud voice from the throne, saying, "Behold, the tabernacle of God is among men, and *He will dwell among them*, and they shall be His people, and God Himself will be among them" (Revelation 21:3, emphasis added).

Over and over again, we read of God's desire to be among His people.

Wasn't this what God sought with the nation of Israel as well, and why He made provision for a tabernacle with them? "'Let them construct a sanctuary for Me, that I may dwell among them'" (Exodus 25:8). By carving out a place on earth, where there was separation from the rest of the world, a place entered by praise and thanksgiving, a place that required atonement at one's first steps, a place of washing and sacrifice through the means provided by the tabernacle, a place of service and ministry to Him, God could uniquely be in the midst of His people as a holy God, even here on earth.

And what about the New Testament? Did we get a downgrade of dwelling in the New? No, what do we see there? Something different? We still see God talking about dwelling in the midst of His people, but Jesus redefines the place where God uniquely dwells: "'For where two or three have gathered together in My name, I am there in their midst'" (Matthew 18:20). This is tabernacle language! Jesus redefined the tabernacle, the temple—no longer to be constructed of brick and mortar stones but living stones assembled in His name! Now, some will say, "But isn't God omnipresent?" Yes, and yet, Jesus is making a distinction. The way Jesus is present in the midst of His people is not the same way that He is present everywhere, at all times.

Of the New Testament temple, the gathering in Jesus' name, the same words are applied:

> [W]e are the temple of the living God; just as God said,
> "I will dwell in them and walk among them;
> And I will be their God, and they shall be My people"
> (2 Corinthians 6:16).

In place of stones, the New Testament temple is constructed as the living stones assemble in Jesus' name. Similarly, we read,

Christ Jesus Himself being the corner *stone*, in whom the whole building, being fitted together, is growing into *a holy temple in the Lord*, in whom you also are being built together *into a dwelling of God* in the Spirit (Ephesians 2:20-22, emphasis added).

And again, we read the same truth in 1 Peter: "[Y]ou also, as living stones, are being built up as a spiritual house for a holy priesthood, to offer up spiritual sacrifices acceptable to God through Jesus Christ" (1 Peter 2:5). The gathering is the new and greater temple, the place where God's Spirit uniquely and manifestly dwells in the midst of His people, who are a nation of priests and Levites ministering to Him. When God says in His word that "you are a temple" (1 Corinthians 6:19), we have projected our individualistic culture onto the whole of Scripture, as if these other passages do not exist. It is true that individual believers are the New Testament temple of God, but it is also true that the gathering is uniquely the place where the individual living stones come together.

The gathering in the New Testament is the new and greater place of separation from this world (i.e., today's tabernacle). It is a place entered by praise and thanksgiving; a place of confession, repentance, atonement, and washing by the water of the Word; and a place of offering sacrifices of praise, service, and ministry to Him (just as in the Old, but better, as now, even a Gentile has become a Levite and priest, able to enter in behind the veil of separation, having been atoned for by the blood of Jesus).

So, going back to the church of Ephesus, Jesus says, "Therefore remember from where you have fallen, and repent and do the deeds you did at first; or else I am coming to you and will remove your lampstand out of its place—unless you repent" (Revelation 2:5). By the way, Jesus doesn't say, "Do the things you did at first." That is a poor translation. Sadly, so many are trying to go back to something they did a long time ago, thinking that's the way forward when that is not necessarily so. That isn't what the verse says. Jesus literally says, "And the first works do." First is not an adverb that indicates the time when things were done. "First" is an adjective describing the works. It's about what Jesus said was to be first, which was of course to love God with all.

These are sobering words, and we should let them sink in. We almost never imagine that Jesus would say something like this, especially to a church doing all they were doing under such hardship! We expect Him to say, "You are doing all these things well, but pay attention to this. Of course, it's understandable that your love has grown cold given the conditions that you have endured. Don't make too much of it. Don't be too disturbed by it." Yet, that is not what Jesus says. Jesus says, "I am so greatly disturbed by it, I will remove My presence from your midst on account of it." He doesn't say, "I want more just like you." More is not the problem. He is saying, "The deadness, the dryness, the lack of love in your heart for Me is the greatest problem!"

Can you imagine Jesus writing letters to churches today and those being heard today the way they were then? How many people would hear Jesus warn about removing His presence and honestly think, "Wait? What presence? I've never noticed You were here. What difference would that make?"

The Church is house-poor in terms of His presence. According to Barna's findings, "Eight out of every ten believers do not feel they have entered into the presence of God, or experienced a connection with Him, during the worship service."[1] In addition, "Half of all believers say they do not feel they have entered into the presence of God or experienced a genuine connection with Him during the past year."[2]

Many who are called by God's name cannot discern the presence or absence of God's palpable presence, and even worse, they don't desire it. How can a gathering belong to Him, be His, and be about Him, if His presence is irrelevant, and worse, if His presence is viewed as a disruptive problem? "God, You being here, doing what You do, gets in the way of the mission!"

The Church has built a dead theology to justify its dead reality. It takes false comfort in the fact that God is omnipresent and concludes that He can't be uniquely present or remove His presence. Even a kindergartener reading the Bible could tell that there is omnipresence and that there is manifest presence all throughout! How dumb! How dead!

What if the Church has been preoccupied with a problem as its greatest problem that isn't the greatest problem at all? And in doing that, what if the Church has made the truly greatest problem devastatingly worse?

What is the greatest problem, the real problem?

We have elevated the Great Commission above the Greatest Commandment.

What if on account of that, we have actually peddled solutions and strategies for the #2 thing that cost us the #1 thing?

Consider this, Jesus never called the Great Commission "great." In fact, Jesus never called the Great Commission the "mission" at all. In Matthew 22, Jesus was asked, "'Teacher, which is the *great* commandment in the Law?'" (Matthew 22:36, emphasis added). Jesus responded saying, "'YOU SHALL LOVE THE LORD YOUR GOD WITH ALL YOUR HEART, AND WITH ALL YOUR SOUL, AND WITH ALL YOUR MIND.' This is the *great* and *foremost* commandment" (Matthew 22:37–38, emphasis added). By including the article, "the," and adding "foremost," Jesus made it clear this is not a great commandment on par with other great commandments, but the greatest commandment.

Yet, we live in a generation of Christianity that insists that the "Great Commission" is our purpose, our priority, and the chief reason that we're on the planet, but God didn't say that. Don't you think it takes great audacity to put words in God's mouth, to see what God said is the greatest and first commandment as less than something else (that He never described that way), and then to label what He never said was the greatest as the greatest and first? It's audacious actually, and we have had to repent for doing the same.

Let's get clear about what Jesus said. When Jesus said, "'Go therefore and make disciples'" in Matthew 28:19, the word that is translated as "go" is actually, in the Greek, "having gone." It is an aorist passive participle. Jesus said more literally, "Having gone, disciple all the nations." The word, "disciple," is in the imperative mood, meaning it is the command of the sentence. However, we have made the command, "Go." When we recognize that the emphasis is on the verb "disciple," which Jesus defines as both baptizing them and teaching them to obey all He commanded, then it makes it clear that what God is after is whole hearts. That is His emphasis, and it's not just hearts that intellectually assent to Him. It's hearts that do what? It's hearts that obey Him (Matthew 28:20).

The Matthew 28 command, to put it simply, is one of the commands of Christ. We once cataloged all the commands of Christ. Grouping like ones together, our list contained 115 commands. The Matthew 28 command is one of them. A command is a command, and yes, it is important, but Jesus didn't say anything different about this command to elevate it above the others.

Imagine if we picked a different command and did the same thing with it as has been done with the Matthew 28 command. Imagine if we wrote a book and said that what Jesus says in Matthew 5:48—"'Therefore you are to be perfect, as your heavenly Father is perfect'"—is the Great Calling or our mission on the planet. You'd throw a flag, wouldn't you? Why? Because what would give us the right to elevate that above the rest of Christ's commands?

Yet, we have allowed the Matthew 28 command to be treated this way and done the same in calling it the "Great Commission." Again, it was not Jesus who said it was the "mission," and it was not Jesus who said it was "great." Do you know who made that term so popular? Hudson Taylor.[3] He was a great missionary, but he wasn't God. He was a man. He is the one who popularized calling it both the "mission" and "great," not God.

Today, the waters of humanism (a philosophy that has replaced the worship of idols with elevating humanity itself to the highest place) have flooded the Church as much as they have our culture. Therefore, should we be surprised that in seeking to reach a humanistic world, the Church has placed the love of man above the love of God Himself, so much so that it has become common for people to equate the second commandment with the first, actually claiming that loving people is the equivalent of loving God? Could the idolatry be more pervasive?

We need a revolution—a revolution that returns to our first love, loving God. Most revolutions exist to take the throne from the King. This revolution exists to return the throne to the King. We need a revolution of radical change, and we need a revolution where the body begins to revolve around its true vertical axis again.

In summary, the problem of the Church is that we have put the "Great Commission" and a love for people above what God actually said is the **First and Greatest Commandment**—to love God. The solution is a revolution that returns to our first love.

How much change would be required to bring about such a first-love revolution? What precisely must be done?

Part II

The Revolution's Repentances

5

Put First Things First

The enemy has damaged everything within the sanctuary.
Your adversaries have roared in the midst of Your meeting
  place;
They have set up their own standards for signs (Psalm
74:3-4).

What does the Church in revolution look like? What must change? What does restoring the Bride to her first love require? It requires the body to begin to orbit around the Lord and what fills His heart—not revolving around what fills the room with people. A revolution in the Church that returns to its first love lives for the attendance of One.

Our elevation of the "Great Commission" over the Greatest Commandment has reoriented nearly everything in the Church from a true north orientation (oriented toward Him) to a skewed orientation (oriented toward people). So, what must change to see a revolution that returns to its first love—loving God with all our heart, soul, mind, and strength? What must happen to remove the idol of jealousy erected in the house of God that has led us to bow to people in place of God? What must be done to restore the orbit of the body of Christ to revolve around Him?

We must make changes in six areas. The first area requires putting first things first by restoring the Greatest Commandment to its rightful place.

How do we do that?

1. Repent and Return to Our First Love

This revolution needs to begin where every revolution in the Kingdom always begins—with repentance. Let's not forget, "[W]e must all appear before the judgment seat of Christ, so that each one may be recompensed for his deeds in the body, according to what he has done, whether good or bad" (2 Corinthians 5:10).

Whereas Protestants have rightly emphasized salvation is not by works but by grace through faith in Christ alone (Ephesians 2:8–9), we have also underemphasized the judgment seat of Christ where believers are judged by their works. (We believe the great white throne judgment before the Father is where all are separated either to Heaven or hell and that only believers [get to] stand before the judgment seat of Christ.) Even for assured believers, we have been warned about that day:

But each man must be careful how he builds on it. For no man can lay a foundation other than the one which is laid, which is Jesus Christ. Now if any man builds on the foundation with gold, silver, precious stones, wood, hay, straw, each man's work will become evident; for the day will show it because it is *to be* revealed with fire, and the fire itself will test the quality of each man's work. If any man's work which he has built on it remains, he will receive a reward. If any man's work is burned up, he will suffer loss; but he himself will be saved, yet so as through fire (1 Corinthians 3:10–15).

On the day we stand before our Lord, we will take radical responsibility for both our action and inaction, but it will be too late to do differently. However, if we take radical responsibility today, things can change. It is not too late. If we repent and seek God's face, there can be a revolution that returns to its roots for the praise of His name.

Where does repentance start? In these urgent days and at this critical hour, it starts with us confessing that the captivity of the Church has taken place on our watch, both as a result of our doing and our omission. We must repent for setting our hearts on God's house being more full of people than full of His presence and for placing people's preferences above His. We also must confess and repent for the ways we have contributed to the giving away of His throne by putting other things in His place.

We must plead for God to do a thorough work in us, because if we don't get down to the root (i.e., the why of what we have done) and only deal with the fruit (i.e., what we have done), the root will produce a crop again. With ears longing to hear what the Spirit says, we must ask, "God, in what ways have I been complicit and a willing participant in Your dethroning? Why did I give Your throne to what the people wanted? What was I trying to secure by pleasing them? Was it prominence? Was it praise? Was it fear? Was it security? Was it satisfaction? Was it significance?" We compromise for what we prize.

We must confess and repent, not just of behaviors but the intent and idolatry in our hearts. Let us set our heart on one thing. A singular prize leads to a singular pursuit. Where our "'treasure is,'" there our "'heart will be also'" (Luke 12:34).

2. Clarify the First and Greatest Commandment as Our Calling

We must stop calling the Matthew 28 commandment the "Great Commission." Jesus neither called it "great" nor the "mission." Why are we so comfortable putting words in the mouth of our Lord that He did not say?

What has happened as a result of us elevating what Jesus did not and deprioritizing what He did? The result has been the Church living with a skewed sense of purpose! Our mission—our purpose and our reason to live—is found in Mark 12:30, "'AND YOU SHALL LOVE THE LORD YOUR GOD WITH ALL YOUR HEART, AND WITH ALL YOUR SOUL, AND WITH ALL YOUR MIND, AND WITH ALL YOUR STRENGTH.'" In Matthew 22:38, Jesus also said about this commandment, "'This is the first and greatest commandment'" (*New International Version* [NIV]). Jesus said that everything that follows flows from this First and Greatest Commandment to love God, along with the second commandment to love others.

For decades upon decades, the focus of the Church has been "in" or "out," "in" or "out." Pastors and teachers have argued with evangelists and leaders over and over and over again.

"In!"

"No, out!"

"In!"

"No, out!"

The primary focus of the Church is neither "in" nor "out." It is up. If you do not get this right, you won't get the "in" or the "out" right. It is of critical importance that we clarify the First and Greatest Commandment as our calling.

And as we do, let us not forget that Jesus taught us in Matthew 28 to make disciples as we teach them to obey all that He had commanded. If we do not teach others to love God with all their heart, soul, mind, and strength, we have not only failed to fulfill the First and Greatest Commandment, but we have also failed to fulfill what we have self-labeled the "Great Commission."

What Jesus said in Luke 10 is often overlooked:

And a lawyer stood up and put Him to the test, saying, "Teacher, what shall I do to inherit eternal life?" And He said to him, "What is written in the Law? How does it read to you?" And he answered, "YOU SHALL LOVE THE LORD YOUR GOD WITH ALL YOUR HEART, AND WITH ALL YOUR SOUL, AND WITH ALL YOUR STRENGTH, AND WITH ALL YOUR MIND; AND YOUR NEIGHBOR AS YOURSELF." And He said to him, "You have answered correctly; DO THIS AND YOU WILL LIVE" (Luke 10:25-28).

Again, we know we are only saved by placing faith in Jesus Christ (Ephesians 2:8-9), but here we see what that faith looks like. A true living faith in Jesus Christ loves God with all and loves its neighbor as itself. The stakes of reclaiming our first love and the First and Greatest Commandment could not be higher.

3. Declare Unashamedly the Ownership of the Gathering—It's His

The gathering is God's. He is the owner. He is the One that everything exists for and revolves around. We need to stop speaking in unbiblical ways about the Church.

It is not my church.

It is not your church.

It is not our church.

It is not the people's church.

It is not the givers' church.

It's God's Church. He is the head. He is the owner, and it's supposed to be the place where His rule is most firmly witnessed here and now!

Along with this, we need to stop speaking in ways that make God the guest of the gathering who is blessed to be in our presence. So often we say to God at the start of the gathering, "God, we welcome You here," but if the gathering is His, who welcomes whom? Who is the guest blessed to be in the other's presence?

We need a revolution, a revolution of love that puts the love of God first again and returns the throne of His house to Him. When we recognize the purpose of the Church is to love God with all our heart, soul, mind, and strength and to teach others to do the same, suddenly the Church looks very different. Suddenly, the emphasis and focus of our questions shift. Suddenly, the offense of the gathering is the withholder, not the "too" expressive worshiper. Suddenly, we move from asking, "Is it comfortable for them?" to, "Is it comfortable for Him?"

We have put people on God's throne, saying the purpose of God is to serve men, rather than keeping God on His throne and saying our purpose is to serve Him. We must no longer bow to the opinions, whims, and preferences of people. We must declare and demonstrate in every way that the gathering is His.

4. Redefine the Success of the Gathering

A revolution that returns to its first love must define the success of the gathering with this single question, "Did God get what God wants from me?" The goal of our gathering is to love God well. What does it look like to do that? If God says it, He sees it. If God wants it, He gets it.

We must stop seeing significance through the lens of a room full of people. Significance is faithfulness in the Kingdom of God. "Did God get what He wants from me?" This question must be our one-and-only measure, and it requires each of us to ask God in advance of the gathering what He wants and to ask God afterward if He got what He wanted.

Believer, do not evaluate a service based on if you were moved but rather on if you moved God. Do not evaluate your church based on whether "good Christians" like it enough to want to stay but based on whether the only One who is actually good likes it enough to want to stay! We have made great concessions in the name of the "Great Commission." Having redefined success, we have lost it. The Church has been under siege by man's priorities, strategies, and activities for far too long. The Church's job is to love God. We must begin to live the mission with every decision.

5. Become a Beyond-the-Line People

A people who love God don't just seek to meet the mandatory minimums (although they do that), but they go beyond the baseline requirements to seek Him and bring Him unrequired offerings. They come into the gathering asking, "What can I do, and what can I give to God that I have never given Him before to bless Him in a way that I have never blessed Him before?"

There is confusion in the house of God today. As we've taken on our culture's anti-striving narrative, we've come to believe that God doesn't desire—and isn't blessed by—sacrifice. Is that Biblical? When God says "'to obey is better than sacrifice'" (1 Samuel 15:22), it has been taken in such a way as to say that God doesn't want sacrifice! What Bible are we reading? One of our own making. God's point is that sacrifice cannot be a cover-up for disobedience. Sacrifice cannot please God in lieu of obedience. For example, "I didn't obey but gave a lot of money instead" doesn't bless or honor God.

God never condemns sacrifice. He even calls us to it (Romans 12:1; Hebrews 13:15). The heart of people who love Him, who go beyond the line of requirement, is echoed in what David said, "'I will not offer burnt offerings to the Lord my God which cost me nothing'" (2 Samuel 24:24). This space of freewill offerings is where the heart of God is truly moved by true love. A first-love revolution says like the Psalmist, "What shall I render to the Lord / For all His benefits toward me?" (Psalm 116:12). We must become a beyond-the-line people reclaiming the space of freewill offerings to the Lord, even reclaiming the place of sacrificial offerings to the Lord. We think that grace, not law, means less. It should mean more. Filled with the Spirit of God, we should be able to do—and have a heart to do—what we could not do before. We need to get beyond mandatory minimums for the One we love.

6. Repent of Idolizing Attendance and Anointing

We need to repent of using God, seeking to steal His throne, and putting ourselves at the center. Depending on the stream we come from, this can be done in two different ways—through the idolization of attendance or through the idolization of anointing. In certain streams, being known as "anointed" comes with great gain (which is why you may get pushed down when they come to town). In other streams, being known for leading a big church does the same.

Both of these idolatries seek His platform to make a statement, not of His praise, but of ourselves, our success, and our strength. This is not that different than showcasing horses and chariots to testify to man's might and impressiveness (Psalm 20:7). It is not any different than Simon the sorcerer (Acts 8:9–24), who saw God as an object to be used for his own greatness to be proved. We should not forget the false promise that led to the first sin: "'[Y]our eyes will be opened, and you will be like God, knowing good and evil'" (Genesis 3:5). The first sin was done in pursuit of a spiritual gift! When God is no longer the apple of our eye, but

His anointing is, we're in a dangerous place. Have we forgotten what God has said? "'I am the LORD, that is My name; / I will not give My glory to another'" (Isaiah 42:8). The attempt to use God for our glory is a wicked thing. We must repent.

How do we know if we have idolized attendance or anointing and turned God into a means to another end? The answer is the secret place and what we do in it. Do we go there at all? When we do, can we detect His presence? Are we actually connecting with Him? Are we simply going through the motions? Do we see Him as a subject to study or as a Person to pursue? Is He the treasure in His Word? Do we seek Him? Do we hunger? Do we thirst for Him? Do we make it our aim to love Him every day? For many, His absence in the secret place is no more concerning than His absence in the gathering. Why? Because we see it as duty, but love is far more than discipline.

Also, as we pursue God in the secret place, we must remember that God is not a fool. He knows when He is being sought in order to be bought, but God will not be used! Any attempts to use the secret place as an advantage, a means to pay for God's favor and grace, will be met by God's humbling hand. We need to cry out in desperation, "God, search me and show me. Strip away all deception. Strip away all false pretenses. I want to love You with a whole heart. Burn away all that is not love for You. Refine me with Your fire to have a greater and purer love for You."

Finally, when our prayers for His power and presence to do what only He can do are met by His refining fire, delay, cost, or loss and then we walk away, we must be honest about what it reveals. It shows our seeking was not of His face, nor for the sake of His glory, but for His power to be at work on our own behalf. We must repent of idolizing attendance and anointing and return to seeking Him in love.

6

Prioritize God's Praise

To love God is to want to be with the One who dwells in the praises of His people (Psalm 22:3). To see a revolution that returns to its first love, we must also prioritize God's praise again.

As a result of our rightly intended emphasis on having our whole lives be worship (Romans 12:1), we've lost a theology of corporate worship. A revolution of first love must regain an understanding and practice of praise that is pleasing to Him.

7. Restore Biblical Worship

When you love someone, you want to please them. What pleases God? Praise—passionate, heartfelt praise that loves Him with all of its God-given strength.

There is no shortage of arguments out there today that claim that worship is a matter of the heart, not external activity. Worship is a matter of the heart—that much is clear in Scripture, but is it only a matter of the heart? On top of God's explicit commands of how to worship Him (that answer this question), consider the fact that God never once goes out of His way to commend external indifference in the place of worship, but He does commend the opposite! Worship is not heartless. It is heart plus.

Furthermore, God's commands and revelation of what blesses Him in worship also make clear that Biblical worship is not a matter of personality or style. God never said, "Worship Me like this if it fits your spiritual pathway and if you happen to connect with this particular musical arrangement." When You are God, You have the prerogative to define how You are worshiped, and God exercises that right in what He commands and what He commends. Biblical worship is God's worship, not our worship. Biblical worship is about what God loves, not about how we are wired.

A revolution that returns to its first love calls for the Bride of Christ to become men and women after God's own heart. We must be those who are out to catch God's attention and make Michals mad again! We must stop turning the commands and requirements for how we worship God in the Psalms and elsewhere into suggestions.

Withholding Biblical worship is sin, and it is one of the most offensive sins to bring into the house of God. We must covenant to do the following:

- Sing songs to God, for God, and that exalt God.
- Obey all God has commanded us to obey regarding Biblical worship.
- Stop making New Testament worship a lower standard than the Old.
- Stop evaluating worship for what it did for me, but instead ask, "God, were you pleased with my personal worship of You?"

We must stop being the sons of Eli who put our forks into the offering and withhold portions for ourselves

(1 Samuel 2:12–17). As we worship at a gathering, all too often we're assuming that God is pleased, because we were simply there, worshiped at all, and gave anything at all. But like the priests then, the portion withheld has only provoked our God, and we have become those who are shocked that God's heart isn't moved by our defected, blemished, and partial offerings.

There is a false understanding in the Church that any time we gather, it is a gathering into the name of Jesus and a false belief that any time we worship, the demons flee. Demons can actually love a worship service, because they are mockers by nature. Wherever there is dry, dead, disobedient worship, demons delight in being there, because our lifeless exclamations, our tied tongues, and our lame bodies all make the same claim, "God, You are not that good, and God, You are not that worthy!" To that, the demons give their wholehearted, "Amen!" But there is, on the other hand, a worship that causes hell to flee. It's when God's people pour out their worship passionately. That kind of worship is one that the powers of hell cannot endure and that they cannot stand.

But why so little passion in the praise of the Church today? The hidden resistance to Biblical worship is not primarily our authenticity or personality. It is self-honor. We cannot honor God while trying to honor ourselves. To expose this idolatry of self-honor, we must ask ourselves the honest questions, "When was the last time I looked foolish for God? When was the last time I did something considered dumb, because it blesses God?"

Although not the point of this book, in early 2023, God invited us to bring Him an offering of a continual assembly of perpetual praise. From that day (March 8th, 2023) forward, we have been continuing in an unbroken gathering of 24/7 worship. As a result of that, many of us began to spend more time in worship than ever before, and something profound started to happen. We began to experience an acceleration of sanctification, an increased pace of heart refining, that went beyond anything we had experienced prior. At first, we were surprised as we did not think of worshiping for hours daily as something that would have such a refiner's fire effect on us; however, we could easily recognize that it did. Yet, we should not have been surprised considering what the Scripture says:

> But we all, with unveiled face, beholding as in a mirror the glory of the Lord, are being transformed into the same image from glory to glory, just as from the Lord, the Spirit (2 Corinthians 3:18).

It is precisely as we behold God that we are transformed from glory to glory! We are now convinced that time spent beholding the glory of the Lord in worship is a greatly underutilized means of grace for discipleship and sanctification.

We need a first-love revolution that restores Biblical worship out of love for God and stops allowing church to be a time hell mocks and Heaven turns its face away.

8. Cultivate a Culture of Testimony

"'And they overcame him because of the blood of the Lamb and because of the word of their testimony'"

(Revelation 12:11). God is most honored when His testimonies are told. We cannot honor God while failing to testify to what we have witnessed Him doing in our lives.

Those who love God want the knowledge of His glory to be spread more than they want a church service for His glory to be short. May every gathering be filled with testimonies that fuel believers with fresh faith, hope, and confidence in God. The accuser's continual accusations against us are overcome by the blood of the Lamb; his continuous accusations against God are overcome by the word of testimony. With the enemy continually whispering in the ear of the Church that God is absent, has abandoned us, and is inactive in our lives and world, we need to restore the centrality of testimony both to honor Him and to help the Bride to overcome.

Do not bury or hide the acts of God in your midst and expect God to be motivated to do more. Honor God by sharing testimonies of His love, His protection, His speaking, His healing, His saving, His power, and His freeing. Take the time to thank Him for who He is and what He has done.

A revolution that returns to its first love must prioritize God's praise in restoring Biblical worship and a culture of testimonies told for the knowledge of His glory.

9. Restore a Theology of Direct Ministry to the Lord

As a result of losing sight of our call to love God first, we've lost sight of the true priesthood of believers. The priests of the Old Testament were not said to minister to man, but they were ministering to God (2 Chronicles

13:10)! We are a nation of priests (1 Peter 2:9; Revelation 1:6), Levites, who have a calling to minister in God's tabernacle (1 Peter 2:5). Yet, we have made our ministry primarily and foremost a ministry to men.

A direct ministry to the heart of God precedes all outward ministry to the heart of others.

- The offering of sacrifices of praises continually (Hebrews 13:15) in the New Testament is in direct context and parallel to the Old Testament priestly service of keeping the fire on the altar of sacrifice continually (Leviticus 6:12–13). That was and is direct ministry to the Lord.
- Praying continually (1 Thessalonians 5:17) is the New Testament parallel to the incense being kept continually on the altar of incense in the Old Testament as well (Psalm 141:2; Revelation 5:8; Revelation 8:3–4; Exodus 30:8). That was and is direct ministry to the Lord.

As the priests attended to keeping the fire on both altars continually, they ministered to the Lord. We, as a nation of Levites, must regain our understanding of priestly service to the Lord in prayer and praise. Do we serve others? Yes. But, that is secondary to our first and greatest calling to serve God directly. Word and deed without presence and power are impotent. Put first things first again. Only when believers regain the understanding that worship and prayer are direct service to the Lord will these acts of service be restored to their right place in our lives.

In the New Testament, there is a word that specifically references this priestly direct ministry to the Lord. It is the Greek verb, λατρεύω (pronounced lat-ryoo'-o).

It's found in Hebrews 12:28 and translated as "offer" in the *New American Standard Bible*: "Therefore, since we receive a kingdom which cannot be shaken, let us show gratitude, by which we may *offer* to God an acceptable service with reverence and awe" (emphasis added).

In total, there are 21 uses of this word in the New Testament, and all 21 instances are about service upward to God. A revolution that returns to its roots restores the understanding of a unique form of ministry and service that is purely upward, direct to the heart of God.

7

Restore the House of Prayer

A revolution that returns to its first love must also honor God for who He is, as He is, by relating to Him rightly in prayer. Prayer says, "God, I love You. I believe You. I need You, and I want Your rule here."

10. Restore Prayer to the House of Prayer

In Matthew 21:13, Jesus said, "'My HOUSE SHALL BE CALLED A HOUSE OF PRAYER.'" Jesus Himself prayed, but we believe we don't need to (as evidenced by our prayerlessness). What does that show about what we believe about ourselves and what we believe is needed?

We need to believe that great ground can be gained in the place of prayer again. Not only can new territory be gained for Him, but what has been gained can be enforced and advanced as well.

When Jesus' disciples asked Him to teach them to pray, what did He say? Did He suggest that prayer was impotent or insignificant? Did He say, "It doesn't matter what you pray. All things are foreordained and nothing is going to change?" Or, did Jesus teach them to cry out to the Father in dependence and desperation that His Kingdom would come and His will be done on earth?

Yet, how much enemy territory remains uncontested on account of our prayerlessness? How much ground are we ceding to the enemy in our families, our churches, our cities, our country, and around the world due to our prayerlessness? Where are the watchmen on the walls seeing and stopping enemy attacks? They are inebriated by self-sufficiency, and in their stupor of complacency, they have permitted breaches on their watch!

Prayer, in love for the Lord who came so that the works of the devil would be destroyed (1 John 3:8), goes to war for His glory. Those who pray from this place do not pray "prayerlessly" as E.M. Bounds used to say.[1] They know that God has demonstrated and declared in His Word that "the effective prayer of a righteous man can accomplish much" (James 5:16) and that "He is a rewarder of those who seek Him" (Hebrews 11:6).

Why then is there so little prayer—and fruit from prayer—in the Church? In part, we do not have, because we do not ask. Also, we do not ask, because we do not want; and we do not want, because we do not believe we need. Drunk on Babylon's wine of self-sufficiency, our prayerless lives and churches declare, "God, we don't need or want what You give." Steve Kilpatrick has been quoted as saying, "Prayerlessness is the pinnacle of pride. When we fail to pray we essentially say to God, I can handle this on my own."[2]

We must repent for our self-reliance, for thinking our skills, smarts, or strategies are sufficient and so great that our efforts and activities require only a sprinkling of prayer. We must repent of thinking—and demonstrating through our prayerlessness—that we did not need Him, His power, or His presence. We must repent of thinking He was not what was needed most. We must repent of not wanting Him and His Spirit above all else.

We must recognize that competence is dependence in the Kingdom of God. We must become a praying church who comes to God as Jesus taught us, living a life of prayerful desperation and dependence upon Him. We must cry out for His name to be made holy. We must cry out for His Kingdom to come and His will to be done. And we must cry out daily, "What are the things of my flesh that need to be put to death today? What are the traps and temptations that can be disarmed in this place? What are Your priorities? What do You want done?"

The gathering needs to be preceded by prayer and prayed for as it takes place. For those interested, here are the pre-service prayer points that we use:

1. Clean the slate. Ask God to search you and show you anything that is standing in the way and repent of those things.

2. Pray for enemies. Most do not do this at all, and among those who do, they often do it last. There is power in praying this toward the top of the list.

3. Inquire. Ask God, "Is there anything You want to be said specifically in the gathering/service?"

4. Inquire. Ask God, "What are we up against in this gathering/service, and how do we clear it?"

5. Pray for leaders. This includes praying for all those who are preaching/teaching as well as the

worship leaders in all ministries. Pray for power, protection from distraction, and fresh fire.

6. Pray for soft soil. Pray that hearts would be ready to receive and be responsive to God, His Word, and the work of His Spirit.
7. Salvation. Pray for salvation.
8. His Spirit. Pray for an acceleration of His Spirit.
9. Worship. Pray for Heaven's worship to happen here (in the gathering) and for every type of testimony for His praise.
10. Revival. Pray for revival.

Restore prayer and return to a revolution of first love.

11. Restore Inquiring Prayer

Those who love God want to be led by God. They trust that He knows best, and like David, they inquire of the Lord. In Zephaniah, God declares that He is going to stretch out His hand against several groups of people. Who makes the list? Among those listed are, "'[T]hose who have turned back from following the Lord / And those who have not sought the Lord *or inquired of Him*'" (Zephaniah 1:6, emphasis added). After that warning, how can we not ask the Lord's direction and wait for His answer before setting out?

Is God ambivalent about our autonomy? The Church has become filled with those who do not inquire, and they justify not doing so based on an arrogant notion—that because God has given us minds, we are to make decisions based on the strength of our logic and understanding independent from inquiring of Him. But, how do we reconcile that with what we are commanded to do? In Proverbs 3:5, God commands us, "Trust in the Lord with all your heart / And do not lean on your own understanding." How can we, as New Testament believers, now having much greater access to be led by the Spirit of God, not even ask God what He wants us to do? How can we, as the sons and daughters of God, be led by the Spirit of God if we do not inquire of God?

For most believers today, the very idea that they could pray and get an answer from God feels out of reach. What a shame! This testifies that we're now living a New Testament reality more devoid of the voice and leading of God than that of the Old Testament saints! We need a revolution that restores the place and practice of inquiring prayer.

12. Restore Prayer Ministry

A revolution that returns to first love has the heart of Habakkuk 2:14: "For the earth will be filled / With the knowledge of the glory of the LORD, / As the waters cover the sea." Do you want that? Do you consider how much of God's glory (His gravity and greatness) is not just unknown today but disbelieved today? In love for Him, do you ache for everyone to hear, to see, and to know that the God of the Bible—who saved, delivered, loved, empowered, rescued, redeemed, restored, and fought on behalf of those who loved Him—is still the same God today? How can we justify allowing the world to lack the knowledge of His glory today? Jesus told His disciples to do the following in Matthew 10:8, "'Heal *the* sick, raise *the* dead, cleanse *the* lepers, cast out demons. Freely you received, freely give.'"

If we care about the knowledge of God's glory, then we have to step up to the plate, do what Jesus did, and do what Jesus said we would do! And we should get real, when the disciples did this stuff (healed the sick, raised the dead, etc.), how did they do it? They laid their hands on people, prayed, and then spoke with the authority that sons and daughters as servants of God have!

This has become rare today and so have the testimonies of the sick being healed, the dead being raised, and the demons being cast away! Ministering in hands-on prayer is a very real way in which those kinds of testimonies are produced, and therefore, a significant means whereby the knowledge of God's glory is spread. All of our gatherings should include direct prayer ministry, but why do we avoid praying in the moment when a need is presented? Why do we avoid ministering in prayer as Jesus modeled and taught? Why do we avoid doing that which took place in the early Church? Could it be that our lack of prayer reveals our lack of belief in who God is?

As Ravenhill referenced regarding Elijah[3], so many cry out, "Where is the God of the Bible?" But where are those who call upon the God of the Bible? Where are those who believe His Kingdom is breaking in? Where are those who pray that God's power would be displayed so that people might see and know the love, mercy, and compassion of our great God and so that His name might be praised? Where is the use of the authority of the believer applied to broken bodies, tormented minds, wounded hearts, and oppressed souls? Where is the praying, the asking, so that His fame, His name, and the knowledge of His glory would be known?

Until we get back to praying, "God we aren't entitled to anything, but for the sake of Your glory, we ask You to raise this man," and until we get back to then saying, "In Jesus' name, walk," we will see very few walk in Jesus' name.

How many more testimonies would be told for the knowledge of His glory if we simply laid hands on people and asked God to do what only He can do right then and there? One who loves Him, one who burns for the knowledge of His glory to fill the earth, will not tolerate any type of testimony being untold in their church on a regular basis.

For clarity, it's worth saying that we approach praying for healing quite differently than most assume. Word of Faith theology has several sub-streams (Dominion/Kingdom Now) that all have a slightly different vernacular and ethos, but all of them believe that healing is part of the atonement, including physical healing, and not just for our eternal bodies, but here and now.

Respectfully, we do differ in beliefs. We hold an "Already/Not Yet Theology" applied to the Kingdom of God breaking into this world in every way, including signs, wonders, and healing. A variety of authors have written on this theology, but for those who are unfamiliar with this teaching, we will provide a brief summary here. This view holds that the prophesied age to come (i.e., the establishment of God's Kingdom on earth) was not what most expected, which was a one-stage fulfillment in which the Messiah would come, bring an end to the present age, and establish the age to come (or the Kingdom of God); rather, it was and is a two-stage fulfillment. When Jesus came, He inaugurated the Kingdom of God, and He will return to bring about the end of this present age and the fullness of the Kingdom of God. As a result, we live in the overlap of the ages, where this present age and the age to come are commingled, where the Kingdom of God is already here and also not yet completely here. As a result, we pray for and experience some of the Kingdom of God here and now but not its fullness.

In line with this, we view healing as a sign of the future we have in Christ breaking into the present, a way in which God testifies to the gospel and the promise we have in Christ Jesus. What this means practically is that when we pray for healing for someone, we pray in faith as it relates to God's character (as we are confident in who He is and what He can do), but we pray in hope as it relates to that specific healing happening here and now. Why? Because we don't believe God's Word guarantees all healing here and now. Of course, we do pray with faith for full healing when and if God reveals by His Spirit that He is going to heal, but, unless He does, we pray in faith in His character and in hope for their healing to happen here and now.

8

Reclaim the Full Counsel of God's Word

The days in which we live are worse than those of Josiah (2 Chronicles 34:14–33). Although we have heard the Word of God read like Josiah did, we have not responded like he did. In place of being torn by the Word of God, we have torn out the Word of God. (Anytime we hear the Word of God, those are the only two choices by the way.) And, in place of ripping our garments in grief, we have ripped out pages in pride. We live in the days of the great devolution of man. For all our understanding, we have none. We have been told, "'MAN SHALL NOT LIVE ON BREAD ALONE, BUT ON EVERY WORD THAT PROCEEDS OUT OF THE MOUTH OF GOD'" (Matthew 4:4). A revolution that returns to its first love will honor the Word of God again.

For far too long, God has been considered a counselor among many. Yet, to say, "I love You, God" is to hang on His every word, believe His every word, and obey His every word. We cannot say, "I love You, God, but I'm not interested in what You have to say" or worse, "I love You, God, but what You say doesn't matter to me."

God's Word has been abused and assaulted by those who claim to belong to the house of God. It has been sliced and diced by some to remove what is offensive, whether in doctrinal belief or preaching practice. By others, there has been a refusal to study it and be subject to it, as if we can bypass the sword of the Spirit with the Spirit.

One of the Biblical words for "curse" is the Hebrew word קָלַל (pronounced kaw-lal'). It means to "be small, light."[1] In other words, it is to "lightly esteem" or "make light of." God used this word when He said to Abraham in Genesis 12:3, "'And I will bless those who bless you, / And the one who curses you I will curse.'"

God was clear that it is no small thing to make light of what He says. Do we know this today? Do we believe this today? It's not our confessions that answer these questions but our obedience or lack of it; it's not simply what we say but what we do. In Exodus 22:28, God commanded us, "'You shall not curse God, nor curse a ruler of your people,'" but when we make light of what He says, we do this very thing.

We need a revolution that honors God's Word as authoritative, inspired, and inerrant again.

13. Get Back to Costly Christianity

A revolution that returns to first love will no longer shrink back the standards of God's requirements to a merely complementary level (i.e., how Jesus makes your life better) or to just a challenging level (i.e., take your next step). Biblical Christianity is neither complementary nor challenging, but costly. The call is to die, every day.

Yet, in our idolatry to have people come to our churches and stay, we have filed the edges off the Bible and cheapened the call of discipleship. We're so impressed with churches that have a lot of people coming, but we should not be. It's not rocket science. At some point, the Church figured out how to run the house of God like a restaurant or any other retail or customer service industry. If you can get high quality (excellence) that fits the taste of most (relevance) at a low cost, you'll be bursting at the seams. (Imagine your favorite steakhouse at McDonald's prices. It would be full when the doors are open too!) It works for churches the same as any other industry.

However, it's not of God! (I, Shane, confess this as one who spent a lot of my life growing ministries really fast, including hitting the top of the "America's Fastest Growing Churches" list.) It's not Biblical, and it's not "working." We see more and more caving, more and more abandoning the faith, and certainly, it is not producing those who will stand through what is to come.

There is a big difference between following God as a leader and submitting to God as God. Leader and God are not synonyms. We have to stop equating them and using them interchangeably. You follow a leader as long as you like where they are going. You follow God even when you don't. Never forget that God is leading us to Golgotha day after day. However, we have trained people for so long to accept Him as leader and forgiver that the nuance of Lord versus leader has been lost, and His leadership is now rejected when His paths lead to cost and loss. We must return to cross-carrying, costly Christianity.

As we do, we must recognize that all of the commandments of God, which He expects us to obey, are summed up in the call to first, love God with all of us, and to second, love others as ourselves. Jesus said in Matthew 22:40, "'On these two commandments depend the whole Law and the Prophets.'" The word "command" is the Greek word ἐντολή (pronounced en-tol-ay'), which literally means "*in* the end" and focuses on "the *end-result* (*objective*) of a *command*."[2] Commandments obeyed out of a dry, dutiful, and dead heart miss the entire point; they do not reach the intended result! We sacrifice for the One we love, and we obey God out of love for Him, desiring to please Him and wanting Him more than any other.

14. Preach the Full Counsel of God's Word

We must repent for adding to and omitting from God's book, attempting to make God more relevant, attempting to edit God, and attempting to give God courses in political correctness. To remove barriers to attendance and make God more palatable, we have filed the edges off what He says, avoided the controversial topics, and preferred to please people with preaching instead of pleasing God as faithful heralds of His Word.

We profess the Word of God is good and the gospel of God is unto life, but then we say, "But not that part, God," as we ignore, lament, or despise certain teachings. We have lost our reverence. We have lost our awe. We have lost our love for God and His Word. How have we become so comfortable darkening His counsel with our ignorance? If God said it is good and for good, why the shame and why the shrinking back from what He has said? We have too many paid professionals in pulpits who neither fear nor honor God.

In our actions, we have said, "God, Your Word is inconvenient for reaching more people, so I'm going to take some liberties to make You more acceptable. You may be less loved, but there are more people. Let me help You put first things first, God." We have become God's PR agents in our pride and idolatry. We must preach the full counsel of God's Word and remove the blood from our hands (Acts 20:26–27).

Those whose first love is God love God and love His every word. There is nothing He says that they will not say. Too often, we assume that if others know that we believe the Word of God is the Word of God, they know what we believe on tough and controversial issues. That's not true. It's not true in our families. It's not true in our friendships. It's not true in our small groups. It's not true in churches. When someone does or shares something that is contrary to the Word of God, and we say nothing, our silence is interpreted as approval and endorsement.

We must understand that in our omissions, people hear what they want to hear. I (Shane) have known many family members and friends who have all attended one of the largest churches in America. My own parents, who are quite conservative, Bible-believing believers, attended it and absolutely loved it. They never had any red flags or concerns but felt challenged by the preaching. My own brother-in-law, also a preacher and pastor, assessed the content of that other pastor's preaching and concluded, "He is solid." However, I was recently speaking with a long-term friend who leads a small group there. He described those living both homosexual and transgender lifestyles attending the church and feeling loved, welcomed, and at home there, but he also shared that after attending for a whole year, they do not perceive they are being called to do anything different.

How can that be? You see, even when pastors have solid theology in their own beliefs, but their preaching never gets practical about what being slaves of righteousness looks like versus living in sin, people interpret all their preaching and principles through their own lens and continue to do whatever seems right in their own eyes. This isn't true of just one sin. It applies to every area of life. Whatever sin a church does not explicitly address in preaching, it will become full of.

When we look at Scripture (both Old and New Testaments), we find that frequently the Word of God lists and specifies what sin is and what righteousness is. Without those specifics, people perceive the preaching as a reinforcement of their own beliefs. We must preach the full counsel of God's Word again.

15. Present the Gospel at Every Gathering

Oddly, most of those who are putting the so-called "Great Commission" above the Greatest Commandment are failing to present the gospel when they gather. In most cases, this comes from our insecurity and feelings of embarrassment if people do not respond. We need to be less concerned about the statement it makes about us and our effectiveness and more concerned about eternity. For others, they do not present the gospel, because they know that the gospel, too, is a hindrance to numbers.

Out of love for Him and others (which is doing what is best for them as God defines it), we need to present the gospel at every gathering and call for a response—clearly presenting the problem of sin and eternal separation from God but forgiveness and salvation by grace through faith in Jesus Christ alone. Be clear that faith is not just in Jesus as Savior, but also as Lord, which means choosing to obey Him and not just receive Him as the forgiver of their sins.

One large church in our region will not give the opportunity for a hand raise or altar call, because it is "undignified." Considering the call to follow Christ requires dying to our own dignity, this should be shocking to us all, but the idolatry has gone that far today. Is the gospel offensive to the flesh? Yes! It requires the death of the flesh daily (Luke 9:23). God does want people to be saved and truly saved, so present His gospel—not America's latest rendition of it—at every gathering.

16. Get Real about Sin

Stop minimizing sin by referring to it with euphemisms such as brokenness, struggle, or something we can do better in. Speak of sin as God does. Speak of sin's cost as God does, and speak of repentance as God does.

Using a euphemism to describe sin is not contextualization. Biblically, contextualization was never compromise, and it was never concession. To say that you can "do better" is not the same as saying something is morally wrong. It certainly is not to say it is an offense against God that requires the blood of Christ to cover. You can "do better" at something without ever having done anything wrong, and you can be better at something without having any guilt.

The way we're talking about sin is undercutting the value of and need for the Savior. These egregious euphemisms need to stop, as does indifference to sin—and blindness to sin—in the household of God. We must consider a single sermon that does not convict of sin and call to repentance a waste of God's time and a failure in the pulpit.

Many believers think that they grow beyond repentance and beyond the need for repentance as they mature, but how does such a belief square with Scripture? It doesn't. There is a progression that often leads to such lukewarmness. When we first come to Christ, we are keenly aware of our need for forgiveness and salvation; however, over time, as God works in our lives, we tend to be seen as good and told by others that we are good. We come to believe that we are, and as a result, we see less and little need for repentance. But are we good? No, God alone is good, and any good that anyone sees in us is on account of God and His goodness. Nearness with God will not deceive us into believing we do not need to repent, but distance from God will embrace such a delusion.

We must call sin and evil by their true names, call for repentance, and then teach people that they cannot carry out their commitments on their own but must rely on God. We must get real about sin and recover the critical role of repentance in the Christian life, which is one of the most foundational practices to grow in our love for God (Luke 7:47).

17. Get Real about Money

Love isn't stingy. We're called to give or give generously (Luke 6:38; 2 Corinthians 9:6–13) and that is impossibly defined as tithing or less than tithing. In the Old Testament, God was clear that tithing was returning to Him what is His and therefore, refusing to steal. Tithing was and is not giving.

Furthermore, the tithe is binding on New Testament Christians. Why? Because the tithe preceded the Mosaic Law and was affirmed by Christ! It's horrible theology to lower the New Testament standard with finances below the Old Testament standard with the simple phrase, "That was Old Testament." And, to do this when the New Testament standard and example is giving (which is beyond tithing), giving sacrificially (which is beyond giving), and even giving all (see Acts) makes this teaching unconscionable!

If Abraham tithed to the priest (Melchizedek) foreshadowing Christ (Genesis 14:20) and that preceded theocratic laws via Moses, then we should be tithing to Christ today as well. If the tithe went to fund the tabernacle of God in the Old Testament (Numbers 18:21–24), it should be given to the tabernacle of God in the New Testament (the Church). After all, the financial demands on a church for local and global mission (loving God with all and teaching others to do the same) are greater per capita than that of the Old Testament temple and its priests, but the body of Christ limps due to stinginess and disobedience here.

Let's get real about money. If people don't trust God with their money, they don't trust God at all. If people won't give generously to God with their money, they do not love Him at all. Get real about money and what it means. Cast mammon off the Church!

18. Get Real about Time

Love and stinginess do not go together and love for God and disobedience certainly do not. If American Christians were to review the requirements of a Bible-believing Christian in terms of prayer, worship, Bible meditation, and serving, they would likely conclude that these requirements are either "extreme" or "impossible." Why? Because so often in the West, Christians are trying to fit Christianity into the same life the rest of the world lives.

How many times do we hear one of the following? "I am too busy to pray. I am too busy to serve. I am too busy to read my Bible. I am too busy to go to church." Being too busy for God and the things of God and loving God are not compatible.

Excessive extracurriculars for kids and students have stolen generational discipleship and made the basic Christian life impossible for an American Christian family. We need to stop forfeiting the call of our faith when given a choice between cultural normalcy or Biblical fidelity.

19. Restore Biblical Humility

In an age of self-promotion, of prizing popularity and platforms, we need to be those who do what the Scriptures say: "Therefore humble yourselves under the mighty hand of God, that He may exalt you at the proper time" (1 Peter 5:6). Sometimes God will initiate a process to humble us, but we should not miss what this passage says. It commands us to choose to stay under His hand.

That is important, because so many people bite back when God's hand comes down.

In a version of faith where Christ is supposed to make our lives better, when times of pressure and pressing come, most believers today quit. God is doing a good work in them, but under the pressure of it, they hit eject. Humility, however, trusts God. It trusts the good that He is up to even when the refining work that He is doing in us does not feel good. It is in that place of pressing that what is in us (and does not belong) is intended to get pressed out of us! When we're pressed down and what doesn't belong doesn't get pressed out, what happens? When we're lifted up, we puff up, that is what!

Trust Him. Do not press eject. Remain under His mighty hand, and remember there is a time that the thing you are convinced will destroy you is actually what God will use to qualify you. If we were preaching, we would repeat that, so, we're going to do the same here. There is a time that the thing you are convinced will destroy you is actually what God will use to qualify you!

Furthermore, we live in a day when God's terms are used but redefined. Love is used but redefined. Faith is used but redefined. The same is true with humility. Today, being humble is equated with being nice and giving deference only. As a result, pastors are encouraged to go along with the majority vote and not take a firm, unwavering stance on what God has called them to do in His Word or by His Spirit, lest they get accused of being arrogant.

Think of the countless times in Scripture that one who was siding with God was viewed as arrogant. In John 9, what do the religious leaders say to the man born blind? "'Give glory to God; we know that this man is a sinner'"

(John 9:24). Today, the same takes place, as those who are arrogant say to others, "Don't be prideful. Don't be resistant. Don't be arrogant. The right and humble thing is to agree with us and give God glory by doing so." However, it would be no more humble today than it was then to agree with them at God's expense.

Biblical humility is not thinking of ourselves more highly than we ought (Romans 12:3), yes, but that is not all there is to humility. Biblical humility is a combination of deference, dependence, and determination. In addition to deferring to others (assuming that deference is done in faithfulness to God), Biblical humility is also dependent upon the Lord. That is why the humble pray. They know they need God. They know they can do nothing apart from Him. In their humility, they are dependent. Humility is not just an aspiration; humility is demonstrated in action—the action of prayerful dependence.

Furthermore, the humble are determined. They are unwavering, unshakeable, and unmovable in their commitment to believe what God said and do what God said. The truly humble will stand alone against an entire nation that disagrees in order to stand in alignment with what God has said. When Moses defied Pharaoh, was he being humble or arrogant? When Hananiah, Mishael, and Azariah refused to bow, were they being humble or arrogant? When Nehemiah refused to come down, was he being humble or arrogant? When Jesus was opposed by virtually every religious leader from every school of thought and had thousands of religious Jews calling for His death, He would not bend. Was He being humble or arrogant?

God does not look—and all throughout Scripture never has looked—upon concessions made at His expense and said of the one making them, "What a humble act by a humble man! What a humble act by a humble woman!" Biblical humility agrees with God uncompromisingly. Love for God agrees with God uncompromisingly. Yet, the idolatry of attendance has perverted Biblical humility into agreement with the majority, compromising at God's expense.

20. Declare Dead Incremental Discipleship

We must declare dead incremental discipleship, because that is what it is. The idolatry of attendance has attempted to change the waters of God into one of gradual entry. Yet, true Christianity calls us to full surrender as the starting line and the standard every step of the way (Matthew 16:24). Having changed the standard of full surrender to be the finish line instead of the starting line, almost nobody arrives at that which Christ said was the start.

Does full surrender as the starting line mean that we will not have more to surrender as we go? No. As God illuminates and calls us to continue to follow Him, He makes us aware of areas of surrender that we had not previously known were areas of withholding. In this way, we are always growing in surrendering more, and yet, also fully surrendered (because we have fully surrendered to what we know). New believers may only know three things that God requires, but if they do all three, they are fully surrendered. For the rest of their faith journey, they will grow in what they know, and as long as they surrender with all new knowledge, they remain at the standard, which is full surrender.

Make full surrender the starting line and the standard again. If a person's baptism wasn't a walk into his/her own grave, then that person has not been baptized. There is absolutely no place for unrepentant sin in the Christian life. If you have people in the church who do not love God with all their hearts, souls, minds, and strength, you have neither fulfilled the First and Greatest Commandment nor the Matthew 28 commandment to teach them to obey all that the Lord has commanded.

We have so many people who, at costly intersections of faith and life, resist "giving up" their lives for God and walking in obedience, because they didn't realize they were already to be given to Him. But Scripture is clear on this:

> I have been crucified with Christ; and it is no longer I who live, but Christ lives in me; and the *life* which I now live in the flesh I live by faith in the Son of God, who loved me and gave Himself up for me (Galatians 2:20).

All Christians give their lives to Christ when they come to Him. As a result, Christ is not a part of our life but "Christ . . . is our life" (Colossians 3:4).

When God calls us to lay down our lives as we go through life, He is not calling us to a new decision but calling us to continue in an already-made decision. The Christian life is the crucified life. It is the resurrection life as well, yes, but so often when we say that, we fail to recognize that resurrection only follows crucifixion.

For far too long, we have not baptized people in the waters of death and resurrection but in the water of blessing and benefit. As a result, we do not have disciples of Christ but bodies in buildings. Out of love for God, we need to declare dead incremental discipleship. That is what it is.

21. Restore Motivation to Believers

We want to please the One we love, and He has said that we cannot please Him apart from faith. What is faith and what does it do? Faith believes that God becomes "a rewarder of those who seek Him" (Hebrews 11:6).

Does the Church have this basic faith anymore? Is the Church motivated to seek God, believing He rewards? No. When everyone is told they get the same no matter what they do (which is not what God says), are they spurred on to seek and sacrifice for God? No.

In our idolization of the presence of people over pleasing God, we have attempted to coddle people and comfort them in their lack of seeking and sacrifice. In so doing, we've killed the theology of motivation in Scripture, a theology that has consequence and reward, stick and carrot. The very basic definition of faith, believing God rewards those who seek Him, is not even intact in the household of faith!

God gave great rewards and great consequences throughout Scripture to motivate His people to seek Him. We must stop catering to those who don't want to seek and start speaking to those who do. Teach people that what they do makes a difference. Teach them that God becomes a rewarder of those who seek Him, part of the definition of faith, and teach them that without faith we cannot please Him. Teach them that we reap what we sow, both from good and from sin. Teach them about a God who judges and who rewards, both in this life and in eternity.

We have so much bad theology out there that says that God always gets what He wants and that what we do doesn't make a difference here or in eternity. The household of God has become filled with unmotivated believers who do not know there is more of God, do not believe God will give more of Himself as our reward if we seek Him, do not realize how much what they do can impact the heart of God Himself, and do not think their inactivity, apathy, and indifference have personal eternal consequence! Yikes!

People may feel loved by what they don't recognize as false assurances now, but they will not feel so loved when they stand before the throne of God. Teach the Scriptures and restore motivation to believers. For those who want to be told they don't need to strive or seek and that their sacrifice-less lifestyles are inconsequential, let them go wherever an ear tickler exists, but do not be one yourself. Your refusal to say what they want to hear will also ignite fresh fuel and fire on the body of Christ.

Do our works make us righteous? No! But our righteousness in Christ does work (Philippians 2:12; 2 Timothy 3:16-17). Believing the Biblical truth that God rewards good works is not contrary to the belief that we're saved by grace through faith alone. A faith that saves is one that obeys (Matthew 7:21-23), and a faith that pleases God believes God rewards. We are not saved by our good deeds, and we are not paid for them, as if we have earned a wage. However, we are rewarded for them. There is a difference. We cannot fail to understand this!

We must get back to heralding Biblical truth. "[F]aith without works is dead" (James 2:26), and repentance requires that we "'bear fruit in keeping with repentance'" (Matthew 3:8). In the same way that we cannot take credit for our salvation (because we acted in response to God's drawing [John 6:44]), we cannot take credit for our works, because they are a result of God working within us (Philippians 2:13).

As a result, our works are not a statement of our righteousness, but they are a statement of God's righteousness. They are intended to shine and bring glory to Him (Matthew 5:16). When we lack works, we rob God of the right response to His grace, the right testimony of His grace, and the right testimony of His righteousness. In short, a motivated believer doing good works is not anti-grace but a true testimony and right response to His grace. The lack of motivated striving, seeking, and sacrifice is actually the great anti-gospel, falsely testifying against the grace of God in our lives.

22. Stop Giving False Assurances

Another manifestation of our idolatry of attendance is the false assurance of eternal salvation we give, caring more about one's presence in our church than one's presence in eternity. Which shows what? It shows that regardless of what we say we are after, we care more about people being comfortable coming to church than comfortable on the Day of Judgment.

Much of what the Church is doing is counting and considering a disciple as someone who intellectually ascents to Jesus as Savior but does not live with Jesus as Lord. Have we forgotten that even the demons believe (James 2:19), and yet, we've called disciples those who do no better than demons?

The standard of faith is not a profession alone. The standard of faith is teaching them to obey all that Jesus has commanded (Matthew 28:20). In Matthew 7:21, Jesus said that saying, "'Lord, Lord'"—which by the way is beyond saying "Savior, Savior"—will not get someone into Heaven but only those who *do the will* of the Father. Jesus speaks of those who know that He is Lord, and who profess Him as Lord with their mouths, as not going to Heaven because of what? They did not *do* His Father's will! To believe in Jesus as Lord you must submit your life to Him.

Make no mistake that the unrepentant do not inherit the Kingdom of God (1 Corinthians 6:9–11; Galatians 5:19–21; Ephesians 5:5; Hebrews 12:14). Any form of deception that says someone is accepted, loved, and therefore can do whatever he/she wants must be denounced publicly and frequently. This is the belief of demons not the faith of daughters and sons. We have become those false people-pleasing prophets saying, "Peace, peace" when there is no peace, considering a profession of faith that does not bear fruit in keeping with repentance as genuine faith in Jesus as Lord. It is not.

Stop giving false assurances. Stop being false prophets. Much blood is on the hands of the teachers of today for this. God is seeking to populate Heaven for His glory, not pack our churches with people for our own praise.

23. Return to Walking by Faith (Not by Sight)

Hebrews 11:6 tells us, "[W]ithout faith it is impossible to please [God]" (God added) and in 2 Corinthians 5:7, we are told, "We walk by faith, not by sight." We do not only begin in Christ by faith, but we also continue in Christ by faith. Faith is not a one-time, initial, past-tense occurrence in our lives. We walk—present tense—by faith, and without doing so, we cannot please God! Those who love God want to please God, and those who want to please God want to honor Him with faith. Yet, there is little walking by faith and a lot of walking by sight in the Church today.

To walk by faith, we have to reclaim the Biblical definition of faith, as there has been both negligence with and assault upon the true definition of faith by many teachers and preachers of today. Faith has been portrayed as determined and wishful thinking by some (i.e., decreeing and declaring whatever is desired), but faith is not something that originates in our own will. Faith has also been portrayed as a relative or friend of doubt by others, but faith is antithetical to doubt.

What does the Bible teach us about faith in a nutshell? First, where does faith come from? "[F]aith *comes* from hearing, and hearing by the word [Note, "word" is from the Greek word, "rhéma," which refers to a spoken word. It is not the word for Scripture, "graphé," nor for Jesus as the Word of God, "Logos."] of Christ" (Romans 10:17, aside added). This means that faith follows God's speaking, whether it's God speaking in Scripture—the word choice above shows the Spirit is required even to be able to receive that—or by His Spirit. We cannot have faith for something that God has not spoken or promised. We can hope for it. We can pray for it. But, we cannot have faith for it. Faith's origin is God's speaking.

Faith, however, isn't just aware of what God has said; it responds to what God has said in a very specific way. "Now faith is the assurance of *things* hoped for, the conviction of things not seen" (Hebrews 11:1). Faith responds with confident assurance—not with wavering or double-mindedness—to what God has said, even and especially when what He has said goes against what our eyes see and our minds comprehend.

So, very practically, what does faith do? What does it mean to walk by faith? When it comes to God speaking through His Word, one who is seeking to honor God with faith reads and believes what He has said, with confident assurance, even when what God has said isn't seen, even when so-called evidence is brought forward that appears to contradict what God says. Faith stands on what God says; it does not fall for what it sees.

When it comes to God speaking by His Spirit, one who is seeking to honor God with faith listens, hears, and tests what has been heard against the Word of God and in the place of prayer. If the Spirit confirms it as coming from Him, faith then partners what God has said with confident assurance, not with wavering. Again, faith stands on what God says; it does not fall for what it sees.

Imagine that all you had was the New Testament, with Jesus so explicitly commanding the disciples when to go, where to go, what to take, what not to take, what to do, what not to do, when to move on, and when to remain. Then imagine reading about Paul, where he was led by the Spirit and where he was prevented by the Spirit from going, on top of all the other instances of God calling His saints with such specificity. Imagine that is all you had (meaning the Bible, but not the conditioning of your experience within American cultural Christianity). Then imagine that you met someone who identified as a "follower of Jesus" but said God had required nothing more of him/her—or said anything beyond—the "Great Commission" that He gave 2,000 years ago. If you had not been inoculated by American Christianity but had fresh eyes, don't you think you'd be a little dumbfounded to say the least? Do we really believe Jesus has changed that much, or is it that we don't want to be led that much? We cannot follow Jesus while not believing and following Jesus when He speaks today.

Walking by faith, being sons and daughters of God who follow the Spirit of God, has been diminished so much that some can even vehemently reject what God speaks, what He promises, and what He calls them to do and still consider themselves faithful while doing so—as if it is not sinning to disobey God's specific directives as long as they are still applying the general truths of God in Scripture to whatever path they have chosen. That wasn't the case for Jonah. It isn't the case for us.

Faith starts with what He says, by His Word and by His Spirit's speaking, believes what He says, and obeys what He says. Don't ever make little of this act of faith, because God doesn't. What did Jesus ask if He would find upon the earth when He returns? Faith (Luke 18:8). What made Jesus marvel in a positive sense? Faith (Matthew 8:10). What made Jesus marvel in a negative sense? No faith (Mark 6:6). What is a gift of God that we can bless

God with, here before we see, but not once we see in eternity? Faith.

Faith, being essential for both salvation and for pleasing God every step of the way, has come under tremendous assault. For those who have perpetuated the attack on faith, whether in teaching that doubt and faith go together or in teaching that faith is an act of our own will (rather than a response to what God has said), repent.

Furthermore, for those who have treated the Spirit's speaking as something to be held loosely versus tested until either rejected or partnered with faith, repent. You cannot love God while not believing Him when He speaks and not walking faithfully according to what He has said by His Spirit. Yet, we live in dangerous days where this is considered the common Christian life.

Without faith, it is not unlikely that we will please the One we love but actually impossible to do so. We need a revolution in which the household of faith walks by faith, Biblical faith, once again.

24. Pass Along a Persevering Faith by Enduring and Embracing Cost

In the Church, there is much emphasis on an initial decision but so little emphasis on perseverance. We should be greatly alarmed by this considering Jesus' warning: "'Because lawlessness is increased, most people's love will grow cold'" (Matthew 24:12).

Is a one-time decision sufficient? Is that what we are after? More importantly, is that what God is after? Is that what is required for one to spend eternity with God? Should we assume that a packed place, full of people who have made a decision, translates to an increased population of Heaven?

Questioning the validity of the numbers present used to be easily dismissed as fear-mongering, but now, the research we've already looked at has revealed it to be a reality. Self-professed Christians in our country by and large believe things irreconcilable with faith in Jesus Christ as Lord and Savior. In many cases, the decision that is being made is not even something that could be called true faith (faith in Jesus who is a consultant that makes my life better or counselor who comforts me is very different than Jesus as Lord), but even where decisions are made with proper gospel presentation, are these seeds being snatched up by the evil one or are they persevering in the faith?

When Jesus said who would inherit eternal life, what did He say? Did He say that anyone and everyone who once made a decision would? No! What Jesus said is this: "'For God so loved the world, that He gave His only begotten Son, that whoever believes in Him shall not perish, but have eternal life'" (John 3:16). Sometimes, we are so familiar with the Scripture that we fail to see what is there. The word "believes" is in the present participle form in the Greek, which means it is literally "the one believing." Jesus did not say that those who made a one-time decision would inherit eternal life. He did not say "those who believed." He said that the one *believing*, the one *continuing in belief*, would.

Add to that what we are told in Revelation. Who will eat from the tree of life? The one "'who overcomes,'" as it is translated in Revelation 2:7, is literally "the one overcoming." It's an active present participle, indicative again of ongoing activity. Who will not be hurt by the second death? The one "'who overcomes,'" as it is translated in Revelation 2:11, is literally "the one overcoming" again. Who will be clothed in white garments and not have their names erased from the Book of Life? Who will be made a pillar in the temple of God and have written on him or her the name of God? The answer is the same: the one "'who overcomes'" as it is translated in Revelation 3:5 and Revelation 3:12, is literally "the one overcoming."

Perseverance matters! Whether you believe salvation can be received and then uprooted or you believe that if someone is ever saved then he/she remains saved, in all Biblical paradigms, the definition of truly saved requires perseverance to the end. Jesus was so clear about this. In Matthew 10:22, He said, "'You will be hated by all because of My name, but it is the one who has endured to the end who will be saved.'" Again, He said in John 15:6, "'If anyone does not abide in Me, he is thrown away as a branch and dries up; and they gather them, and cast them into the fire and they are burned.'"

Perseverance, in Scripture, is absolutely essential:

[Y]et He has now reconciled you in His fleshly body through death, in order to present you before Him holy and blameless and beyond reproach—*if indeed you continue in the faith firmly established and steadfast, and not moved away from the hope of the gospel that you have heard* (Colossians 1:22-23, emphasis added).

Perseverance's significance cannot be overstated, and it is not a minor theme. Among the numerous other verses that speak to it are the following:

- "[B]y which also you are saved, *if you hold fast* the word which I preached to you, unless you believed in vain" (1 Corinthians 15:2, emphasis added).
- "*If we endure*, we will also reign with Him; / If we deny Him, He also will deny us" (2 Timothy 2:12, emphasis added).

In short, a "yes" needs to remain a "yes" if one is to be truly saved. Jesus warned us in Matthew 10:33, "'But whoever denies Me before men, I will also deny him before My Father who is in heaven.'" Despite Jesus' clear warning, some are teaching that self-professed atheists who made a decision as a teenager are still headed to Heaven. This is false assurance!

The pressures of secularism will pale in comparison to the times of tribulation to come. We must raise titans of the faith who persevere to the end. Are we passing along a faith that perseveres? Are we passing along a faith that is able to persevere in what is prophesied to come? Do we love our God to the extent we want Him to have a people who have faith when He returns? Do we love our God to the extent we want Him to be glorified with a people whose love remains white-hot for Him even in the face of profound persecution and loss of life? Or are we fine passing along a baton of faith that won't stand when pressing and persecution comes? Jesus asked if He would find faith on the earth when He returned. The absence of faith on the earth should be a heartbreaking contemplation for all who love Him.

Passing along a faith that stands to the glory of Christ in the last days cannot be done by knowledge transfer and aspiration alone. We cannot pass along what we do not possess. Therefore, we must be those who are not caving or avoiding cost with concessions ourselves. We must be those who are not caving to preserve significance, satisfaction, or security. If we shy away from cost and consequence, that is what we will pass on to them. If we tolerate untruth in the house of God, that is what we will pass on to them. If we are lax, loose, and unfaithful with the Word of God, that is what we will pass on to them. If we do not operate in the power of the Spirit, but in the might of man, that is what we will pass on to them. If we water down Biblical faith, equating it to belief alone, which even demons have, that is what we will pass on to them.

We live in a day and age where a persevering faith that endures and embraces cost and consequence will have testimonies to tell of faith costing us jobs, positions, and more. Our young people need to hear those testimonies, and they need to hear how God faithfully provides despite the costs and consequences as well. We cannot pass along what we do not possess.

We need a revolution that passes along a persevering faith by enduring and embracing cost and consequence.

25. Stop Reinventing and Marketing a Jesus Made in Our Own Image

Everybody loves Jesus, not the historical Jesus, not the real Jesus, but the one they've made in their image. Today, it has become very popular to promote a Jesus who exists for our blessing and our benefit. He is made to be ambivalent about areas of grey, which are not truly grey but are portrayed that way. He is pictured as being comfortable in the presence of unrepentant sinners but not in the presence of religious zealots. He is portrayed as soft-spoken, mild-mannered, and tolerant (with tolerant misdefined to mean endorsing of everything). This Jesus is not demanding but is willing to be accepted on any and all terms. Does this Jesus sound familiar? Jesus has been popularly portrayed this way, but the problem is that the Jesus who is being promoted is not Jesus at all. As the Israelites fashioned an idol of their own making and declared it to be the god who led them out of Egypt (Exodus 32:1-4), so this Jesus of today is an idol that has been collectively fashioned and had the label, "Jesus," slapped on it.

Yes, Jesus came for sinners (us), praise God (Mark 2:17)! But, let's not be dishonest about who God is. Those sinners in Jesus' midst were all repentant. He loved sinners and called them to repentance (that is what love does, by the way). He did not keep company with the unrepentant, clapping them along on their way into another day apart from Him and certainly not into an eternity apart from Him. Jesus was accused of being a friend of sinners, but He confronted them on His first encounter with them.

Jesus did not teach grace as tolerance toward sin, but He said anyone who relaxed the least of the commandments and taught others to do the same would be called least in the Kingdom of Heaven (Matthew 5:19). Jesus did not reduce the requirements of the Law, but instead taught a higher bar, obedience not only of action but in heart and thought (Matthew 5–6). Jesus did not teach us to take our sin lightly but warned that we should pluck out even our eye or cut off our hand should it cause us to sin (Matthew 5:29–30). Jesus didn't teach giving acceptance and approval to young people for whatever they thought was best, but He taught that anyone who caused a young person to be led into sin would have been better off if drowned in the depth of the sea (Matthew 18:6). How does the Biblical Jesus fit with the ever-increasingly popular version of Jesus? He doesn't.

Jesus is Lord. His sword is very sharp. He brought to the world, among other things, much more illumination and revelation about hell that awaits the unrepentant. He is coming to judge the living and the dead. His fiery eyes of judgment are being kindled and His winnowing fork is already in His hands.

In many cases, both the leaders of the people of God and those who identify as the people of God have been complicit in this redefinition of Jesus, just like Aaron and the Israelites with the calf. All too often, we have picked and chosen the parts and pieces of Jesus' life and teachings that are culturally acceptable and concealed the rest of Him and what He said. We've done this in pulpits. We've done this in our personal lives, and we've done this in parenting.

This audacious idolatry to fashion Jesus to our liking is so wicked, it has created a depiction of Jesus that is full of half-truths and deception and called it, "Jesus," to get more people to accept Him. This is not love for Him, but an act of hatred born out of our idolatry.

We need a revolution where Jesus is faithfully represented and His words faithfully heralded by those who truly love Him for who He is, who are proud to serve the God of all mercy, compassion, love, truth, justice, and judgment so that those who hear of Him faithfully love Him as well.

26. Get Rid of Gross Grace

In our attempts to appease people instead of gain the approval of God, we've made grace gross. Grace is for change; grace is not for staying the same. Remaining in the sin Jesus died for is not a testimony of grace; it is a gross distortion of grace. Any reference to grace as being okay with sin is exactly what Hebrews 10:29 warned us of:

> How much severer punishment do you think he will deserve who has trampled under foot the Son of God, and has regarded as unclean the blood of the covenant by which he was sanctified, and has insulted the Spirit of grace?

We call tolerance and endorsement of sin, "grace," and on account of that, we've inoculated a nation to seeking God, saying, "He's fine with you just the way you are." But is that true?

Romans 15:7 has been translated as, "Therefore, accept one another, just as Christ also accepted us to the glory of God." From there, many have read into the word our cultural concept of "being accepted just the way we are" and as a result, have twisted the meaning of grace toward licentiousness. In truth, the word translated as "accept" means "to draw to oneself,"[3] something that makes sense in the context of the circumcised and uncircumcised being united in the church of Rome. Translations that read "receive one another" come closer to the original text. Therefore, taking this verse to mean God accepts us—or that we should accept each other—in unrepentant sin is a gross redefinition and perversion of the word. (Some translations use "accepted" for the verb form of grace in Ephesians 1:6, which would be more literally translated as, "to the praise of the glory of His grace, which He *graced* us.")

In making grace gross, we now have a nation of lukewarm Laodiceans who think they are rich when they are poor, think they can see when they are blind, think they are clothed when they are naked, and think they hear when they are deaf. And, one of the most lamentable realities is that our pastors have led us into such a state.

How can we who died to sin still live in it (Romans 6:2)? We cannot. Do we all sin? Yes. Do we all fall and fail? Yes. Is there any room for self-righteousness in Christianity? No. What do Christians do? They genuinely repent and strive to turn away from sin and toward the Lordship of Christ. We do not live in or condone unrepentant sin. We need a revolution that gets rid of gross grace.

27. Return to Fear of the Lord

The Scripture testifies, "The fear of the Lord is clean" (Psalm 19:9), but we have made the fear of God a dirty thing. By and large, in the Church, the fear of the Lord is absent in both our preaching and practice, and when it is preached, it is redefined to merely mean "reverence." Is that a complete and right definition of the fear of the Lord? Acts 5 answers the question. Right after God strikes Ananias and Sapphira, we read, "And great fear came over the whole church, and over all who heard of these things" (Acts 5:11). Did their fear mean reverence alone? Of course not. This was a group that was meeting daily and devoting themselves to the apostles' teaching, the breaking of bread, and prayer (Acts 2:42,46). They were already reverent, yet, when they saw sin come with a consequence, they feared the Lord.

We have taught teddy bear theology to the point that people do not even fear God anymore. Yet, Psalm 147:11 says, "The Lord favors those who fear Him." However, His pleasure is a small thing when the goal is people's pleasure instead.

It has become quite popular for pastors to portray the lion as a cub and to speak of the fear of God as a curse rather than a cure. But what does God say about fearing Him? God says in Proverbs 14:27, "The fear of the Lord is a fountain of life, / That one may avoid the snares of death." Also, He says in Deuteronomy 10:12–13,

> "Now, Israel, what does the Lord your God require from you, but to fear the Lord your God, to walk in all His ways and love Him, and to serve the Lord your God with all your heart and with all your soul, *and* to keep the Lord's commandments and His statutes which I am commanding you today for your good?"

All throughout the Scripture, we see the truth that the fear of the Lord leads to life.

Sinning unrepentantly or affirming that which God calls evil is nothing less than a complete lack of fear of the Lord. Our God is merciful. He is patient. He is waiting and longing for repentance. But, He also will not contend with man forever. God's patience is not permission. We serve a God who is just. We reap what we sow. He is long-suffering and slow to anger, but He does get angry, and apart from repentance, there is sure judgment.

Restore the fear of the Lord—not faux fear, which runs away from the Lord, but true fear, which runs toward Him. What difference does restoring the fear of the Lord make in our gatherings? It has more implications than we can articulate here, but when the Lord is feared again, we won't see the King being treated casually.

Everyone knows that if we were invited to the White House to meet the president, we would prepare, arrive in advance, and communicate honor in our words and actions, even if the president was our own father. Yet, when we go to God's house, there is far less honor shown. In the quest for seeker sensitivity, we have turned the guests into god and made everything revolve around them. In wanting our "guests" to feel comfortable, we've told them anything is acceptable in God's house as long as it is authentic. Along these lines, we've communicated (directly and indirectly) that lateness, ambivalence, indifference, and unrepentance are not problems. What does all that communicate about our God and His greatness?

When we are meeting with someone important, it shows. If someone who knew nothing about a gathering came to our gathering and observed it from start to finish, what would they conclude about the One whose name the gathering is in? When we fail to prepare, strolling into the place of God's manifest presence without repentance, assuming God is good with the fact that we are physically there (but acting as if He does not care about the state of our heart), there is a lack of the fear of God. When we come late (or when pastors do the same), coming for the part of the gathering that is preferred or deemed a "value add to me," there is a lack of fear of God.

When God is feared, people come early, not late, and they stay late, not leave early. He is the priority. The day is planned around Him. When God is feared, people plan their dress so as not to be restricted from a single Biblical command in the place of His praise. When God is feared, man's own preservation of dignity drops, and it shows in worship and in response to the teaching of His Word.

We need a revolution that returns to the fear of the Lord.

28. Hold Holiness in High Regard Again

When we turn from sin we say, "God, I love You most. I want You most. There is nothing better than You." That is why those who love Him above all else hold holiness in high regard.

Angels are so wildly impressed with the holiness of God that those who surround His throne (and have their whole existence) cannot stop crying out, "'HOLY, HOLY, HOLY'" (Revelation 4:8). And consider this, the angels are blown away by His holiness despite the fact they have never sinned. That tells us that God's holiness is not just the absence of sin but the presence of an infinite, immeasurable goodness that overwhelms even sinless creatures!

Yet, the Church has become embarrassed by the holiness of God and His standards of holiness. Let us love His holiness and long to reflect His holiness in our lives. True Biblical holiness is only possible through the power and presence of God, and when believers walk in freedom, they will do so in great humility knowing they are dependent upon God to overcome. False holiness is self-righteousness— behavior modification with a prideful, evil, and self-reliant heart. That is no holiness at all. True holiness makes a statement about Him, not us. True holiness is born of humility, which both knows the depths of its sin and hungers for more of God. James 4:6–8 (summary added) explains it:

> But He gives a greater grace. Therefore *it* says, "God is opposed to the proud, but gives grace to the humble." Submit therefore to God (Humility). Resist the devil and he will flee from you. Draw near to God and He will draw near to you (Hunger). Cleanse your hands, you sinners; and purify your hearts, you double-minded (Holy).

Holiness is not a matter of insignificance. We must hold holiness in high regard again. We must do what 1 Peter 1:16 commands: "[B]ecause it is written, 'You shall be holy, for I am holy.'"

29. Strive Again

It's become popular today to say, "I don't need to strive or beg. I'm a son/daughter. The Father's kids don't do that." It's a popular sentiment, but popularity and prevalence don't make something Biblical.

Romans 15:30 says, "Now I urge you, brethren, by our Lord Jesus Christ and by the love of the Spirit, to *strive* together with me in your prayers to God for me" (emphasis added). The word for "strive" is a combination of two words, σύν (pronounced soon), which means "with" and the verb, ἀγωνίζομαι (pronounced ag-o-nid'-zom-ahee). This verb is constructed from the noun, ἀγών, which originally meant a "place of assembly," then a "place of contest" or "stadium," and then the "'contest' itself."[4] The significance of this is that "the verb has the same shades of meaning as the noun."[5]

All that to say, we must stop this anti-sacrifice and anti-striving nonsense and strive again. Love sacrifices for the one it loves. We've made our relationship with God a one-way relationship, where only He sacrifices for us, and we never sacrifice for Him. This anti-striving message is unbiblical and like much of what has gotten off course, it too is born from the place of saying what itching ears want to hear.

Is Romans the only place that we see the call to strive? No! Colossians 1:29 says, "For this purpose also I labor, *striving* according to His power, which mightily works within me" (emphasis added). Colossians 4:12 reads,

> Epaphras, who is one of your number, a bondslave of Jesus Christ, sends you his greetings, always *laboring (i.e., striving)* earnestly for you in his prayers, that you may stand perfect and fully assured in all the will of God (emphasis and translation added).

In addition, Mary, Tryphaena, Tryphosa, and Persis are commended in Romans 16 as those who "worked hard." This is literally from the word, kopiáō (which is the verb form of kópos, meaning "exhausting labor"). Today, these four would not be commended but corrected!

We have few who would be willing to sacrifice their life for their faith with a gun to their head, but even fewer who would actively sacrifice of their own volition without a gun to their head. Pastors can't work even 5 full days a week anymore without worrying about their health or having others do so. This is because they sacrifice to an idol of attendance, and the success, significance, and security it brings to them, instead of sacrificing to the God they love. When we strive in our own strength and do not walk according to the Spirit, we can't even do more for God than the average person does for his/her own benefit. What a false testimony!

Cost, loss, and carrying the cross have become foreign words to American Christianity, so much so, the very presence of them will often lead to accusation: "Surely you did wrong to experience wrong." Others will simply think you are crazy, because you are willing to suffer loss. At other times, you will wish for a word of encouragement and find the silence deafening. When you do, remember that cost is not a native tongue of man. It is a tongue of the friends of God to say, "I know it came at a cost," and that language is only learned as you pass through the land. Those who have not paid a cost cannot have compassion on those who have. Don't grow faint-hearted but strive for Him again, knowing that He sees and rewards everything given, sacrificed, or lost for His name and the gospel.

We need a revolution that strives again for the One it loves. Strive in step with His leading, in the freedom of defining success rightly as faithfulness, and according to His power (Colossians 1:29). Step into a life of sacrifice again.

30. Put a Base on That Balloon

For those who have come from the Spirit stream of Christianity, a revolution is gravely needed as well. Those who seek to follow the Spirit, without the Word, are like unanchored balloons blowing in the wind.

According to research done by the Cultural Research Center of Arizona Christian University and released by Dr. George Barna in 2022,

> [A]bout half of all Pentecostal and charismatic pastors believe that good people can earn their eternal salvation (47%), reject the notion that success in life is consistent obedience to God (45%), and believe that earthly wealth is provided by God to people to manage for His purposes (46%). Nearly half (45%) do not believe that human life is sacred while almost half embrace the idea that having faith matters more than which faith it is.[6]

The neglect of God's Word in the pentecostal and charismatic streams of faith is not only costing them the Word but also the Spirit.

A first-love revolution prioritizes what God says both in His Word and by His Spirit, and it recognizes that the Word of God is the only authoritative and inerrant revelation of God by which every word purported to be of the Spirit must be tested and interpreted. If the pastor and the people are not daily reading, reflecting on, and responding to the Word of God, then repentance and a revolution are needed. So many moves of God have drifted off course due to Biblical illiteracy and lack of Biblical fidelity. We need a revolution.

31. Reclaim the Biblical Definition of Love

You have probably heard that the best lies are as close to the truth as possible. We know the enemy is the father of lies (John 8:44) and is certainly happy to speak bold and blatant lies anywhere they might be received. However, he knows not many will accept him saying, for example, that murdering is good. It's too blatant. That is where deception comes in.

Our capacity to discern the enemy's deception has been brought to naught by not obeying even the black-and-white things of Scripture. As a result, the enemy's most effective lies have ransacked the Church, and not only did we fail to recognize it, but we helped him. How? In many ways! But when it comes to how we talk about love, we have helped him the most.

You see, the best lies are not as close to the truth as possible. Those are really good lies, but they are not the best lies. The best lies, the very best work of the enemy, in terms of their efficacy to deceive, are when the truth is stated but a lie is meant. The very best lies are when a statement is made that is 100% true in its wording, but the terms have been redefined in such a way that the opposite of the truth is meant. This is what has happened with the word, "love."

Today the Church is filled with those who are saying, "God is love. It's all about love. The only thing we have to do is love. Jesus said it all comes down to love. It's not our job to judge. It is our job to love." Much of what is said is almost lifted out of Scripture verbatim, a true statement. However, the terms have been redefined to be a completely false statement. What is meant by what is said regarding love today is that we should accept people just the way they are. We should not judge them, and by that, what is meant is that we should not tell them they are sinners, what sin is (as God defines it), and that without repentance from sin, there is no forgiveness, and they will be left in their sin and unsaved for all of eternity.

The definition of love that Satan has sold to the Church is a complete lie meant to lead the Church into an impure and lawless state. Should we be surprised? We know when the Antichrist comes, he will establish himself in the temple of God, which is the Church, and that he is called the man of lawlessness (2 Thessalonians 2:3–7). The spirit of lawlessness is already at work in the Church to prepare the way for the man of lawlessness. This redefinition of the word, "love," is one of his finest works to roll out the red carpet for himself.

What is love according to the Bible? Love is doing what is best for another as God defines it. The perverted and Satanic redefinition of love, which is being promulgated in the pulpits and by God's people, does the opposite of what is actually loving. It condemns itself in what it approves, sending the message of approval explicitly or by its silence. What we call love is nothing other than clapping those along who are coasting down the societal stream when the calamity ahead makes Niagara Falls look like a leaky faucet. That is not love. It is hate.

What is loving? Imagine standing there beside another on the Day of Judgment when the things done on earth, in mind, heart, soul, and body will be judged. We should remember what Scripture teaches about that day. Among other things, we are told:

- "So then each one of us will give an account of himself to God" (Romans 14:12).
- "[B]*ut wait* until the Lord comes who will both bring to light the things hidden in the darkness and disclose the motives of *men's* hearts" (1 Corinthians 4:5).
- "[W]e must all appear before the judgment seat of Christ, so that each one may be recompensed for his deeds in the body, according to what he has done, whether good or bad" (2 Corinthians 5:10).
- "God will bring every act to judgment, everything which is hidden, whether it is good or evil" (Ecclesiastes 12:14).
- "'[I]t will be more tolerable for *the* land of Sodom and Gomorrah in the day of judgment than for that city (the one rejecting the gospel)'" (Matthew 10:15, definition added).
- "'[E]very careless word that people speak, they shall give an accounting for it in the day of judgment'" (Matthew 12:36).
- "God will judge the secrets of men through Christ Jesus" (Romans 2:16).
- "[T]he present heavens and earth are being reserved for fire, kept for the day of judgment and destruction of ungodly men" (2 Peter 3:7).
- "[T]he dead were judged from the things which were written in the books, according to their deeds" (Revelation 20:12).

It is on that day that Scripture will be proven true. Those who continued in unrepentance, while believing their so-called faith profession would save them, will discover that they will not inherit the Kingdom of God. Those who barely escape the flames (1 Corinthians 3:15), because they did not build with precious materials, but with wood, hay, or straw, will have no excuse.

Imagine that day and being there as a witness to another's judgment before Christ. Will that person look at you then and say, "What you did was the most loving thing. What you said was the most loving thing. You prepared me well for this moment. You really did do and say what was best for me as God defines it!" There are many who have others' blood on their hands for what they have given approval of, and while they have done it claiming to do so out of love, it is no love at all. It is truly hatred.

Love does what is best for another as God defines it. A revolution of first love will love God by telling people what is true, what leads to life, and what leads them to love Him with all their heart, soul, mind, and strength, not by telling people what they want to hear.

32. Give Glory to God, Not the Vessel

The priesthood of all believers reclaimed the understanding of God's grace flowing to and through all believers in the form of spiritual graces. However, God does not get the glory when the vessel takes ownership over the grace! In 1 Corinthians 4:7, we read, "For who regards you as superior? What do you have that you did not receive? And if you did receive it, why do you boast as if you had not received it?"

Yet, so many talk about their gifts as if they were not received, as we walk around saying, "My gift, my gifts." Nothing is ours. His grace flows through us, to others, for His glory. The Church has become filled with gravy bowls who think they are the gravy! The grace that flows through and to us is not ours, and it is not who we are, it is Him flowing through us as a vessel.

This distortion of spiritual graces has led to the Church being filled with much more ambition to develop our giftedness than there is hunger to seek God's face in the secret place. What is it that brings God glory and changes hearts? People encountering Him. We need less polishing and perfecting and more seeking and depending. What makes us useful to God? 2 Timothy 2:20–21 says,

> Now in a large house there are not only gold and silver vessels, but also vessels of wood and of earthenware, and some to honor and some to dishonor. Therefore, if anyone cleanses himself from these *things*, he will be a vessel for honor, sanctified, useful to the Master, prepared for every good work.

Useful vessels are set apart for Him and set apart to Him.

In taking the teaching of spiritual gifts and reorienting its intent, which is God's glory and praise, there is far too much talk about "my craft" in the Church today. Paul said he refused to come with eloquent words, but in power, so that faith would not be in human wisdom (1 Corinthians 2:1–5). Most believers have no idea what "coming in power" even means today, and that is not good.

When we say, "That's not my gift. I'm not going to do that," we often insult the grace of God by insisting the grace of God is a hindrance to our obedience. We must stop doing things that only fit with "our gifts." We must stop disobeying, because the service God calls us to is not the one of our preference. When God calls upon us to serve, we say, "Yes," trusting Him to supply what is needed.

Spiritual gifts have become one more me-centric thing in Christendom, and now we have too many specialists and not enough generalists, not enough servants, willing to do anything. We need a revolution in the Church, that all things revolve around Him and all things are unto Him.

9

Be Sons and Daughters Led by the Spirit of God

A revolution that returns to its first love stops rejecting God by utterly refusing, ignoring, and denying the Holy Spirit of God.

The Church slams the door in the face of the Holy Spirit and claims it can do so in love for God, because it still obeys the Scriptures generally as it vehemently rejects God, the Holy Spirit. The rejection of His Spirit's speaking and leading is the cause of many lampstand-less, so-called churches that think they are gathering in the name of Christ but are not. You cannot utterly reject the calling, leading, and speaking of God and love God. Period.

33. Destroy Decrescendo Christianity

Stop justifying dead realities with dead theologies. The notion that Christianity was meant to start off with a bang and be a big giant decrescendo of the presence and power of God until His return is false. What did Jesus say? "'Truly, truly, I say to you, he who believes in Me, the works that I do, he will do also; and greater *works* than these he will do; because I go to the Father'" (John 14:12). A lack of God's manifest presence and power is cause to get on our faces in humility and cry out for what we lack.

Often, we attack when we lack and others have. However, an abundance of God's manifest presence and power somewhere else is not cause for jealousy and attack but humility and hunger. Your theology may be better, but His outpouring in that place is not necessarily a stamp of His approval on their theology. The Lord responds to seeking. His promise of being found is only toward those who seek (1 Chronicles 28:8; 2 Chronicles 15:2; Jeremiah 29:13; Hebrews 11:6). Seeking is the activity of love, the activity of faith, the activity of hunger, and the activity of humility. Sometimes those who have the most hunger and seeking do not have the best theology. Learn to recognize what God responds to most. (However, to be clear, God will never bless or dwell in a place that calls evil good, or good evil, that changes darkness for light and tolerates sin (Isaiah 5:20), or that teaches against the essential doctrines of historic orthodox Christianity.)

We cannot love God with all of who we are and reject Him every time He draws near! When God's manifest presence begins to come into the midst of His people, the Church will see people encounter Him powerfully, signs and wonders will come, and miracles will begin to break out in His presence. Do not turn Him away! Do not say, "No," to His working in your midst!

It's His house and if so-called "disciples" prefer God's absence over His presence and His inactivity over His works, they are not disciples of Jesus Christ. Stop saying they are good people. Rejecting God, the Holy Spirit, is a wicked and evil thing to do. And, if they say, "I'm fine knowing about God, but I don't need to know Him in that way," think of what that says. There is so much of God they are willing to just not know. What does that say about their hunger for Him and of their love of Him?

We are not invited into a relationship to be mere historians but to be sons and daughters of God led by the Spirit of God. When Jesus came in the flesh, He taught the timeless truths of God, and He also came with signs and wonders and deliverance and healing. When Jesus comes by His presence into the gathering today, He does the same, but many will call these things a distraction, saying, "Let's get back to Jesus and the 'Great Commission.'" They have turned the Bible into God's cage, preferring He remain in history rather than come and lead them today. That is not love. That is not discipleship. To justify the rejection of the Spirit He gave, the primary gift of the age in which we live, is not love; it is hatred.

God is the one who said in Zechariah 4:6, "'Not by might nor by power, but by My Spirit,' says the LORD of hosts." How much more should this be the case in the New Testament age in which we live? We need to ruthlessly evaluate where our source of strength is today. Recently, I (Rebekah) was preaching at one of our gatherings. God called for a response, and a group of people came forward to the altar to get free of strongholds and chains that had bound them for decades. As I looked at their faces and the tears streaming down, I felt the desperation of the moment. For them to come to get from God what only God could give and not receive and not get free would be a tragedy, because it would be an anti-testimony. I was broken and desperate and prayed, "God, I need Your power. We need Your power. God, I am poor in power. I need You to pour Your power in, and for Your power to flow out." I have continued to pray that prayer time and time again. Our prayer for more has to be born not just out of a love for people but out of a love for God. Is every testimony we read about in Scripture being told today? If it's not, God is being robbed of what He deserves, and we shouldn't be afraid to confess our lack and cry out to Him. After all, Jesus said, "'Blessed are the poor in spirit, for theirs is the kingdom of heaven'" (Matthew 5:3).

We need a revolution that believes Jesus, believes Him when He said that we will do greater things, and seeks God to do these things in our midst for the praise of His name! Do we realize that God has prepared good works for each and every believer (Ephesians 2:10)? How many of those works will come to pass? Not many if we continue to champion decrescendo Christianity. So many say, "I would love to see something, anything, from the Book of Acts happen here and now!" Believer, how has that become our aspiration and aim? Isn't that a relatively low bar considering we serve the same God who spoke the Scriptures? What if we stopped praying, "I'd like to see something from then happen here and now!" and, what if we started to pray, "God, write a story for Your glory, even here and even now, that is thicker than the Book of Acts!"

We need a revolution that destroys decrescendo Christianity.

34. Teach What God's Word Says about His Presence

What makes a palace a palace? Is it the magnificence of the place that makes a palace a palace? Some do think so, but no, a palace is about residence. It is a palace if the king lives there. We've confused the magnificence of a church with the magnificence of the place, the magnificence of a program, the magnificence of a personality, or the magnificence of the quantity of people present. The magnificence of a church was never meant to be those things. The magnificence of the ekklesia is the presence of the One whose house it is. What makes the Church a church and the gathering a gathering? The same. The King's presence.

For far too long, we have failed to teach what God reveals in His Word—that while He is omnipresent, He also makes His presence manifest. We must stop using God's omnipresence as justification not to seek His manifest presence. When we, as people, believe we have all, we do not seek more. By teaching people that we have all of God's presence (omnipresence), we have inoculated them from seeking more of His presence (manifest presence).

Even Old Testament saints knew the truth that so many New Testament saints are ignorant of today—there are gradations to glory and percentages of His presence. When David sinned, what did he pray? "Do not cast me away from Your presence / And do not take Your Holy Spirit from me" (Psalm 51:11). Was this a prayer for God to not remove His omnipresence? No, David was pleading, "Do not take Your manifest presence away."

On account of our false and failed teaching of this reality, we have injected and infected members of the body of Christ with deadening discouragement and heart-arresting apathy. There is no longing, and there is no seeking, because why seek when you already have?

We have been complicit in redirecting people's hearts toward the pursuit of adulterous affairs with lesser and lower things that they have come to falsely believe will satisfy, will not run dry, and are not in short supply. God is everywhere, yes, but God also draws near. We need—and must desire—the manifest presence of God.

35. Seek His Face! Become a People of His Presence!

In Psalm 105:4, we are exhorted, "Seek the Lord and His strength; / Seek His face continually." How many of our gatherings have this aim? In how many of our gatherings is He not only sought but found?

Recently, I (Rebekah) received a vision of people going to a grocery store, but when they arrived at the store, the shelves were empty. There was no bread, and all that the people received at the grocery store were food stamps. I also heard, "Ruth 1:1," which says:

> Now it came about in the days when the judges governed, that there was a famine in the land. And a certain man of Bethlehem in Judah went to sojourn in the land of Moab with his wife and his two sons (Ruth 1:1).

Full stop. That is what was received. As we prayed for interpretation, here is what we came to understand. In the days of the judges, everyone did what was right in their own eyes (Judges 21:25). And because there was no bread in Bethlehem (which literally means "house of bread"), the people of God went where to get food? To Moab. As a reminder, the Moabites were the descendants of Lot's daughters, who took matters into their own hands and became pregnant by assaulting their father. In short, the Moabites were a symbol of self-reliance, and what we see in this verse is that God's people, in their lack, did not turn to God in dependence but journeyed into self-reliance for provision.

Ruth 1:1 could very well have been written to describe the state of the Church today. The Church, intended to be the house of bread, has no bread. Like the store with no bread giving food stamps instead, the Church has become a place with no bread, a place where Jesus is not encountered and His words are not consumed. Instead the food stamps of principles—principles of self-reliance—are passed out by pastors. Where is the bread—the bread of His presence (John 6:35) and the bread of His Word (Matthew 4:4)? And where are those who feed upon it? We need a revolution. We need a revolution in the Church today.

We are to be a presence people. How can we love someone more than anything and not want to be with him/her more than anything? We can't! When choosing between God's presence and people's presence, a revolution of first love must choose God's presence every time. The age of the Church is simultaneously the age of the Spirit! Yet, in the idolatry of putting people over His presence, much of the Church has lost its lampstand, and much of the Church is on a path to doing so.

A revolution that returns to first love must covenant to consider any gathering without His divine presence an abomination devoid of witness and worthy of great grief. It must covenant to seek His face and wait upon the Lord until He comes. Bring revolution as you determine that if your church service can be successful without God's palpable presence, you've got a problem. Better yet, consider His presence worth dying for every single day.

Why does God come? Why does He stay? What repels Him? God dwells in Heaven, but He dwells here when the things done in Heaven happen here. We have too much of a "do here what we cannot do there" mentality. Those who want Heaven to happen here do the things of Heaven here. What are those things? God does not leave us guessing but speaks plainly in His Word. His presence and power follow purity. In Isaiah 59:2, God says, "But your iniquities have made a separation between you and your God, / And your sins have hidden *His* face from you so that He does not hear."

We cannot seek God's face while doing what He promises will cause Him to hide His face. And no, God has not changed either. We are told explicitly in the New Testament that our actions can grieve Him. God says in Ephesians 4:30, "Do not grieve the Holy Spirit of God." We can also resist Him (Acts 7:51) and even quench the Holy Spirit (1 Thessalonians 5:19).

We have forgotten who the Holy Spirit is and that our actions matter to Him. What we do can please Him and what we do can provoke Him. Holy Spirit is not a proper noun or a name of no significance. Holy is an adjective. The Holy Spirit is . . . holy, and He is more sensitive to sin than the purest conscience you've ever met.

With Jesus, what do we see? "John testified saying, 'I have seen the Spirit descending as a dove out of heaven, and He remained upon Him'" (John 1:32). Can the Holy Spirit find a place to rest and remain when we, in our continuing sin, are shooing Him away perpetually? The Holy Spirit does not rest in a nest of unholiness and unrepentance. The Holy Spirit is deeply disturbed, offended, and agitated by our sin and our tolerance of it. We cannot make light of HOLY-ness and have the Holy Spirit manifest in our midst.

How can we say we're set on seeking God's face and waltz into His gathering with indifference as to whether or not we encounter Him? How can we say, "I want You and want to be with You" while actively building walls and barriers through pride, unrepentant sin, and hard-heartedness? How can we say that we want to be with One whose commands we treat as considerations? He says, "Forgive," and we are unmoved, maintaining we are justified in our unforgiveness. He commands us to love our "'enemies and pray for those who persecute'" us (Matthew 5:44), but we say, "He doesn't understand how great the offense is." He says, "'Seek My face'" (Psalm 27:8). We sit back and slouch in indifference. He tells us that He dwells in the midst of the praises of His people, yet, we want Him to thank us for our presence in the midst of His praises, even as we ourselves withhold His praise.

Seeking God's face actually means seeking His face—it involves searching, looking, thirsting, pursuing, tearing down anything and everything that stands in the way, waiting, and only resting once His face is found. How many of us come to a gathering like this? How many of us lead the people in our gatherings to do this?

A first-love revolution restores the Church to be those who say, "*When You said*, 'Seek My face,' my heart said to You, / 'Your face, O Lᴏʀᴅ, I shall seek'" (Psalm 27:8).

36. Lead People to Hunger for What They Do Not Have

We need to repent of self-righteousness, which believes that we have all of God there is to have and does not believe we need more of Him. The satisfied and satiated do not seek. When you believe that you have all, you don't pursue more. For far too long, the Church has believed that it has exhausted the inexhaustible God. How is it that we have come to think so highly of ourselves and so lowly of Him? A revolution that returns to our first love must long for the One we love, hungering and thirsting like the deer panting for a stream of water (Psalm 42:1), and it must stop saying it makes no difference whether we do or don't.

We live in a day and age obsessed with fairness—defined as everybody getting the same thing, even if they don't do the same thing. That is no fairness at all! Is God unjust? Does God say throughout His Word that everyone gets the same thing no matter what is done? He doesn't. What does He say? In Matthew 5:6, Jesus said, "'Blessed are those who hunger and thirst for righteousness, for *they* shall be satisfied'" (emphasis added). Does Jesus say everyone will be satisfied? No, He says those who hunger and thirst for righteousness will be satisfied. Similarly, in Matthew 5:8, Jesus said, "'Blessed are the pure in heart, for *they* shall see God.'" Does everyone see God? No, the pure in heart are those who see!

When God begins to move, so often He blesses the humble, hungry, and holy (who have done exactly what these Scriptures say), and Christians take offense. Why? On account of their self-righteousness, God's selectiveness is offensive. The idea that someone else is getting something they are not, because someone else is doing something they are not, provokes the flesh. In response, all too often, pastors then placate people in place of presenting the truth that what we do matters.

To quench the Spirit, quench people's thirst. To hinder the Spirit, hinder people's hunger. Tell them that what they do makes no difference. Tell them they already know and have all of God there is to be known and had, and that is exactly what you will accomplish! The most deadly lie to a life of seeking God is believing that you have all of Him there is to have.

There is always more of God to be had, always. He is infinite. We never get to the end of Him. If we believe that we can comprehend all there is to understand and know all there is to know, we have made a god of our understanding and created a god no bigger than our brains. When we think we have it all, we know but one raindrop compared to the ocean of who God is.

Where there is no hunger and no thirst, the people of God do not come to the well for a drink and the body of Christ becomes that dead, dry, and dusty thing that is an anti-testimony. Call Christians to come hungry and thirsty again. If there is a lack, if they recognize their soul is dry and dead, if they have no hunger nor thirst for Him, tell them to take no rest in seeking God until God sets their soul ablaze for Him again. We have nothing if we don't have Him.

37. Stop Saying "No" to New

At the end of Matthew 8, a whole town came out to meet Jesus, and of all the things they could have wanted Jesus to do for them, what did they ask? "[T]hey implored Him to leave their region" (Matthew 8:34). Why? Jesus' presence was a disruption to their lives! Do we recognize that the same is being asked of Jesus in the Church today?

Throughout Scripture, we see that our God is a God who does a new thing. Go figure, the infinite God is not limited to routine! Yet, so often when God acts outside the box of what He has done before, what does He encounter? He encounters annoyance and rejection on the part of His people, and He encounters the same from those who lead His people, as they take a pass on what God is doing in order to maintain their misplaced power base.

We cannot say, "No," to the things of God and love Him at the same time. If God is doing a new work, how do we love Him? By embracing the new work, thanking God for His grace, and testifying to what He is doing! Yet, so many times when God begins to move in miraculous ways, people bury the testimony. Why? They would rather be ashamed of God's activity than be ashamed to believe in supernatural things before men.

How have we justified rejecting God and His works? Sometimes, people will say, "We need to get back to the 'Great Commission,'" but do you see what is broken in that thinking? How can you teach people to love God with all their heart, soul, mind, and strength, while teaching them to say, "No," to Him at the same time? You can't! That is to make a son of hell, not a son of God! Other times, we dismiss what God is doing by saying, "Let's just get back to Jesus. This is a distraction." But, God doesn't act to distract. He acts to draw attention, and that is what He is worthy of receiving from us when He does.

When Jesus came in the flesh, He performed signs, wonders, and miracles while also preaching and teaching His costly and countercultural message. Today, when He shows up, He does the same. When people respond to what He is doing, writing it off as a distraction and saying, "Let's get back to Jesus," what do they mean? They mean, "Let's study about how people should have followed Jesus when He came," but they miss that they are being invited to do that very thing now! So often they will say, "Surely I would not have responded to Jesus in that way," even as they are responding to Jesus in that way today.

The Bible was meant to introduce us to Jesus, not to contain Him in history only. Yes, the canon is closed, but God is still on the throne. God is still alive. God is still active. God is still speaking. God is still working. Yet, when Jesus shows up today, people want to send Him back to the Bible as if it's His cage saying, "Stay in there. Stay in history. Don't show up and do that kind of stuff here and now and distract us from studying You."

What a shame! God has not done everything He will ever do. There are still things no eye has seen, no ear has heard, and no mind has conceived that are on the horizon and ahead of us. All of those things will be Biblical. All of those things will be consistent with the Word of God, consistent with the character of God revealed in the Word of God, and consistent with the ways, will, truth, and message of God revealed in His Word. Yet, none of those things will be things we've ever seen.

Have we considered the full implications of putting God in a cage in this way, believing He cannot do anything other than what He has already done before? If we believe we have to have precedence (i.e., God having already done the exact same thing)—rather than consistency (with God's character, will, ways, and truth as revealed in His Word)—for something to be Biblical, where does that leave us? Where does that leave us regarding God speaking to new topics of today such as abortion or assisted suicide? Where does that leave us in regard to the new things He wants to do in this generation? A Bride that loves God does not say, "No," to God!

Jesus said about the Spirit, "'The wind blows where it wishes'" (John 3:8). Is this our posture? Are we those who say, "Holy Spirit, wherever You wish, whatever You want, and whatever You want to do!" How many born of the Spirit are instead putting up windbreaks in their lives and in the dwelling place of God? When we say, "No," to the Holy Spirit this is precisely what we're doing. There was an ancient form of architecture in Persia (and still found today) that put up wind towers that reached high into the sky to catch the wind and funnel the wind down into the house for the refreshing of those present.[1] We cannot control the Spirit, but we can posture ourselves to receive the winds of the Spirit, to go where the Spirit is going, and to move with the wind!

38. Stop Despising Prophecy

1 Thessalonians 5:19–21 says, "Do not quench the Spirit; do not despise prophetic utterances. But examine everything *carefully*; hold fast to that which is good." Prophecy

is being despised by the Church today and not only in the places you would expect. It is being despised where it is absent, yes, but also where it is prevalent.

In some charismatic and pentecostal streams, people still rattle off prophecy like they are an Old Testament prophet or New Testament apostle saying, "Thus says the Lord." This unbiblical portrayal of New Testament prophecy has opened the door for spiritual abuse to the point prophecy has become despised in many churches.

Another way to despise prophecy where it is prized is to handle it with imprecision and liberty. When people do this, they deliver a blend of something God may have actually said, along with every prejudice, opinion, soap box, snap judgment, and whatever else came to their mind at a particular moment. Prophecy is meant to be the most precise of instruments, the scalpel, but it is currently being practiced in the least precise manner as if a garbage disposal.

The practice of prophecy has become so imprecise in many streams, it's nearly impossible not to despise it. Much of this imprecision has been done in the name of experimentation. After all, many will say and teach, "How can you learn to prophesy unless you just start doing it?" (Can we get the base on the balloon again?) This imprecision with prophecy has also come from the false belief that any time we open our mouths, God will just fill it! (Again, this is a balloon without a base. There is a time when the Spirit bubbles up, and at that moment, it's true—when we open our mouth, He fills it—but to just assume that anytime we open our mouth He fills it is really bad practice.)

Receiving a prophetic word in a house that practices prophecy in this way is dangerous. It's like guzzling down what someone's four-year-old made in a blender without knowing what was put in there in the first place! Trying to sift out something that was actually from God from the mishmash of everything else that was permitted to flow out of one's mouth makes it impossible to hold a prophetic word in high regard. Even the most discerning of individuals would be hard-pressed to untangle this mess!

We need a revolution of love that honors God by embracing His speaking and by practicing prophecy within Biblical guardrails (so that it can be prized and not despised). How can we do that? Here is a simple method that will keep the guardrails in place to protect what should be protected.

When a person believes he/she is hearing something from God, he/she should not share it with another unless expressly led. When someone is expressly led, or at least thinks that is the case, he/she should share in three steps. We first learned of this way to accurately talk about prophecy in reading Bill Jackson's book, *The Quest For the Radical Middle*. These three steps have been only slightly revised from his original model (revelation, interpretation, and application)[2] to received, interpreted, and applied.

Step 1: Received

In this step, the person should share exactly what was heard, how it was heard, and how strongly it was heard. Nothing should be added. Nothing should be omitted.

For example, "I heard/saw this phrase or picture. (This is <u>what</u> was heard). It came in the form of a thought/vision/impression/other. (This is <u>how</u> it was heard.) I would say it was somewhat faint, like a 3 out of 10. (This is <u>how strongly</u> it was heard, or otherwise stated, is a way to prophesy in the measure of faith given [Romans 12:6].)"

Step 2: Interpreted

Most often, the one receiving the prophetic word will not be given the interpretation as well. Therefore, most often, the person prophesying should not try to interpret it. This is usually an overstep and often where prophecy comes off the rails.

God gives a spirit of revelation to some, but He gives a spirit of understanding and/or wisdom to interpret and apply to others. However, if the one who received does believe that God has provided the interpretation as well, he/she should share what was received first, then come to a full stop, and then share the word of interpretation/understanding.

Most prophetic words today are being delivered as a combination of what was received and the person's interpretation (usually the interpretation is wrong). Yet, because they were not separated, the one receiving the word cannot extract the gold from the coal. Separate these, and the majority of mispractice with prophecy will cease.

Step 3: Applied

Beyond a word of revelation and a word of understanding/interpretation is a word of wisdom to apply. Again, a person should only share this if he/she believes that God spoke it. God usually does not give one person the revelation, interpretation, and application. However, if someone truly believes He has, that person should be sure to keep each part separated for the sake of the one who is receiving the prophetic word and their process of testing it, interpreting it, and applying it.

Finally, someone sharing a prophetic word should be sure to say what is true: "You have to test this and see if the Spirit confirms it." Even if God speaks audibly to the one who heard the prophetic word (and yes, sometimes He might), that still is not a word of Scripture for that other person. The recipient must do what Scripture tells them to do, which is not to receive a prophetic word and hold fast to it without testing it first. That person must test it, and it only becomes binding once he/she has received confirmation from the Lord that it is truly what He says.

This is a good three-step process for sharing a word when expressly led. However, if you are receiving a prophetic word from another, what should you do to prize and not despise prophecy?

Step 1: Record

Record or write down exactly what was shared. If someone sharing with you does not follow the steps above, ask him/her exactly what was heard, how it was heard, and how strongly it was heard.

Step 2: Test

Scripture tells us, in the context of prophecy, to test everything and hold onto that which is good (1 Thessalonians 5:21). We have far too many who are holding words loosely but have not tested them and come to the point of full faith or full rejection. That is unbiblical, and it despises prophecy. Test the word in prayer. Ask the Lord if

He, in fact, spoke this: "Is this from You, Lord?" He usually will confirm it with peace. If you have partial peace, ask God if there is any part of it that was from Him. If you do not receive confirmation that it was from Him, ask God if it is a word that can be rejected. If God confirms that, dismiss it and move on. If you don't hear anything, hold it loosely and keep coming back to it, seeking God's confirmation either way.

Step 3: Reject or Partner with Faith

If God confirms it, then you partner His speaking with faith—confident assurance. Faith believes Him. Covenant to keep the word in front of you and continually nurture faith for it.

Step 4: Participate

God's promises require participation in most instances. He speaks to be heard. Every word of God is meant to lead us into a response. Ask God what He wants you to do (how to apply it) to be faithful to what He said. God has promises, and He has paths to those promises. His promises require participation.

10

Revise Leaders, Structures, and Systems

A revolution that returns to its first love must get rid of unbiblical leadership, structures, and systems that reinforce the old idolatry.

39. Restore Biblical Church Leadership

You can't ensure God is the focus of a church and the gathering if structures empower and reinforce the attenders of a church as the owners.

Get rid of unbiblical structures in the Church by restructuring and restoring the role of elders to the true elders of the Church, those senior-most pastors who are truly overseers. (Elder, pastor, and overseer are used interchangeably in Scripture.) Stop separating responsibility from authority by placing people in positions of decision-making power who do not carry the calling or weight of responsibility of a Biblical elder/pastor/overseer. Restore the pastor to the role of head elder, with those around who hold the responsibility over the ministries of the church as the other true Biblical elders.

Build a governance structure with accountability, but do not remove the authority or responsibility of the elders to set direction and follow the Lord. Do this as a particular church or come under the authority of a church that does. Without this, few Timothys will be able to be faithful to God and keep their job simultaneously, because most churches will lose "customers" when they join the revolution and make God the center . . . at least for a while.

40. Stop Measuring Success by Attendance and Budget Size

We must stop measuring success by attendance and budget size. These inevitably redirect the focus to size, quantity, and prevalence in place of presence, purity, power, and God's praise.

Do not tie lead pastor performance to these metrics. Instead, look at what God commends and corrects in Scripture as a guide for your lead pastor evaluation. Look at Jesus' letters to His churches in Revelation and look at what Jesus modeled as He raised up ministers. When Jesus sent out His disciples, He said the following:

> "If a man of peace is there, your peace will rest on him; but if not, it will return to you. Stay in that house, eating and drinking what they give you; for the laborer is worthy of his wages. Do not keep moving from house to house. Whatever city you enter and they receive you, eat what is set before you; and

heal those in it who are sick, and say to them, 'The kingdom of God has come near to you.' But whatever city you enter and they do not receive you, go out into its streets and say, 'Even the dust of your city which clings to our feet we wipe off *in protest* against you; yet be sure of this, that the kingdom of God has come near.' I say to you, it will be more tolerable in that day for Sodom than for that city" (Luke 10:6–12).

Jesus didn't hold the disciples responsible for other people's decisions. He held them responsible for their faithfulness and obedience.

As you seek to evaluate the pastor, look also at the epistles and the commendations and corrections there as your guide. Measure those qualitative things, because whatever you measure is what will matter. Do not measure the two things that no church is ever commended or corrected for in Scripture. It's unbiblical, and it reinforces the idolatry of putting a (false) measurement of the "Great Commission" as the number one thing in place of love for God and single-hearted loyalty to do what pleases Him as the top priority.

Now, many will reference Acts 2 as their paradigm for equating attendance as ministry success. After all, we're told in verse 41, "[T]hat day there were added about three thousand souls." However, there are a few things about that day that are worthy of your consideration before you jump headfirst into defining a church's success on attendance.

For one, what did Peter say leading up to that? Peter said to them:

"Repent, and each of you be baptized in the name of Jesus Christ for the forgiveness of your sins; and you will receive the gift of the Holy Spirit." . . . And with many other words he solemnly testified and kept on exhorting them, saying, "Be saved from this perverse generation!" (Acts 2:38-40).

Did Peter cut out cost, remove barriers, make concessions, or pitch an incremental gradual entry form of discipleship? No.

But also, keep in mind that what is celebrated as the biggest numerical growth day of the New Testament people of God recorded in the Bible was simultaneously the greatest day of numerical decrease in New Testament history. Whereas the estimated counts for Pentecost are just that—estimates, and so we won't try to take a stab at the numbers, we do know that Jews from all the surrounding nations traveled in for the festivals, and the population and crowd sizes swelled tremendously. What that means is that on the day three thousand received Christ, it was also the day that tens to hundreds of thousands of Israelites were no longer counted as true children of Abraham!

We should celebrate when God does a new thing and many say, "Yes," but statistically, those who said, "Yes," on that day were nominal in comparison to those who said, "No," and walked away. In short, start measuring the activity of Acts 2:42–47 and not just measuring overall attendance based on verse 41. In truth, verse 41 was not an overall attendance count. It was a decision count! So, measure decisions (not attendance) and the rest of what is celebrated in verses 42–47, and you will then be basing your ministry data philosophy off Acts 2 in a correct way.

We need a revolution that keeps first things first, defining success in terms of the wholehearted devotion of His people. We must prioritize measuring that, or we'll skew our pursuits to a false definition of success.

In the wake of these worldly scorecards, we've raised up a generation of worldly ministers, performing for pay. It's not wrong to receive pay. After all, we know what Scripture says,

> The elders who rule well are to be considered worthy of double honor, especially those who work hard at preaching and teaching. For the Scripture says, "You shall not muzzle the ox while he is threshing," and "The laborer is worthy of his wages" (1 Timothy 5:17-18).

Clearly, paying pastors isn't wrong, but what is wrong is when pastors would not do what they are doing if they were not paid. (Contrast that to Paul who continued in ministry even when he had to make tents to pay the bills.) When ministry becomes like any other job, doing duties for a wage, versus seeking the face of God and serving as a sent one of God, we have a major problem. Pastors, when your "job" becomes something other than seeking to love God and lead others to do the same, your job will tend to become your god and something you'll even protect from Him, meaning, something you won't sacrifice for Him. That is the problem.

We now have too many paid professionals in the pulpits. Much damage has come on account of the paid ministry mentality. We need to reclaim recognition that ministry is mercy. It is being a slave in the joyful service of the One you love. When ministry becomes a professional transaction, the joy is lost as entitlement sets in. God and His rewards are not one's earnings. Entitlement and service are incompatible. If what you are doing is leading to a sense of entitlement (a "right" on account of your sacrifice), you have lost sight of God and who He is. He is your God, and He is your praise.

Something I (Shane) have done from my early 20s when God sent me into a very high pressure and high accountability ministry environment (and I recommend others doing) was to regularly ask myself honestly before God, "Am I willing to lose my job to be faithful to God?" It takes an honest heart check to know whether you are bowing to your paycheck, the security of the job, the significance of the role, or remaining a true servant of Christ.

41. Stop Perverting His Platform

Those who serve God do not possess a platform. The Church is God's platform. Yet, the Church is filled with shameless self-ambition and sickening self-promotion. It has become a medium for building celebrity. This is not by God's design, and it is not what God has in mind. God is longing and looking for those who say along with Paul,

> I have been crucified with Christ; and it is no longer I who live, but Christ lives in me; and the *life* which I now live in the flesh I live by faith in the Son of God, who loved me and gave Himself up for me (Galatians 2:20).

We must stop talking about our platform, our gifting, and our brand for the sake of our name, our fame, our story, and our praise. When we attempt to use God for our self-promoting purposes, we are no different than Simon the Sorcerer who was exhorted, "'[R]epent of this wickedness of yours, and pray the Lord that, if possible, the intention of your heart may be forgiven you'" (Acts 8:22).

We should remember that God is neither a fool nor deceived. He will judge not only what we have done but also why we have done what we have done. With sobriety, we should, at all times, remain aware of our future reality, the day that we will stand before Him, and all that we have done will be evaluated (1 Corinthians 3:10–15).

God knew—and God knows—that in the heart of every person is the pride of the flesh that is tempted to make what is intended to be about His name, fame, and glory about its own name, fame, and story. He lovingly gave us spiritual practices to crucify the flesh. One of these is the practice of secrecy. As Christians, we need to ask ourselves, "When was the last time that I served God in complete secrecy?"

We need a revolution where those called into service by God serve Him as nameless and faceless slaves, seeking His—and only His—praise to be on attenders' lips.

42. Give the Rod and Staff Back to the Shepherds

We must correctly define shepherding (pastoring) again. Shepherding has been turned into a picture of scratching sheep bellies and being nice, nothing more than modern customer service perverted.

There are two tools of a true Biblical shepherd—the rod and the staff. One is for warding off wolves. The other is for leading the sheep. (Neither of them were back-scratching nor petting devices.) Expect shepherds to lead the sheep and expect shepherds to be ferocious fighters toward everything that brings harm to the pure and spotless Bride. Paul wrote, "What do you desire? Shall I come to you with a rod, or with love and a spirit of gentleness?" (1 Corinthians 4:21). That was not Paul saying he could come like a shepherd or not like a shepherd. Both were within the shepherd's toolbelt.

Who is the Chief Shepherd? There is only One, and we are to emulate His shepherding in every way:

Therefore, I exhort the elders among you, as *your* fellow elder and witness of the sufferings of Christ, and a partaker also of the glory that is to be revealed, shepherd the flock of God among you, exercising oversight not under compulsion, but voluntarily, according to the *will* of God; and not for sordid gain, but with eagerness; nor yet as lording it over those allotted to your charge, but proving to be examples to the flock. And when the Chief Shepherd appears, you will receive the unfading crown of glory (1 Peter 5:1–4).

The question for pastors must not be, "Does the way I shepherd conform to and meet the cultural expectations of today?" The right questions are, "Am I doing what Jesus did? Am I matching the model Christ gave? Does what I say match and sound like what Jesus said? Does what I do match and align with what Jesus did?" If not, we can call what we are doing shepherding, but it is not shepherding. It is a weak, anemic, and pseudo substitution of shepherding that has neither love for God nor love for others (i.e., doing what is best for others as God defines it) at the center but simply a love for ourselves and our own comfort.

We need a revolution that recaptures the true tools of the shepherd from the clutches of customer service so that the undershepherds lead the flock as Christ Himself leads His flock.

43. Go Beyond a Sliver on Sunday

God's standard in the Old Testament was for an entire day to be devoted to Him (Exodus 20:8-11). Clearly, He did not think that was too much to ask or that He wasn't worthy of that. God knows His worth. He knows His value. Do we?

In Acts 20, we read about a gathering that went on all day long until midnight! "On the first day of the week, when we were gathered together to break bread, Paul *began* talking to them, intending to leave the next day, and he prolonged his message until midnight" (Acts 20:7). Today, however, if the service is two hours long, we think that's asking way too much. The early Church in revival met daily (Acts 2:46). Every revival has done the same since. Many in the Church would not want revival today, because they don't want to gather in the Lord's name more than they already do!

To meet people's wants (out of our idolatry of attendance), we have scrambled to have the biggest hour on Sunday, and in doing so, we have even killed off Wednesday night and Sunday night worship gatherings. We've traded qualitative excellence in discipleship—teaching others to love God with all of them—for quantitative excellence on an hour on Sunday, filling His Church with half-hearts for the sake of more bodies. The Sunday gathering in the Lord's name has been shrunk down to an hour and 15 minutes or less, because people don't want to be there very long. Also, the Church wants to rotate the worship center three or four times, because that is the best economic model to get as many people as possible. It's also the worst model to honor God, devote ourselves to the Lord on the Lord's Day, seek His face, and let Him be the leader in His gathering.

We have a nation of Christians who don't know the manifest presence of God, because they have never stayed until He arrived! Moses said, "'If Your presence does not go *with* us, do not lead us up from here'" (Exodus 33:15). But, all too often in the Church, we're saying, "We're not going to wait for You to get here."

As it stands now, people plan so many other priorities on Sunday that they feel the need to get up and run out of the worship center as soon as the pastor says, "Let's pray." Why was God's gathering bookended with something else and His gathering left to get somewhere else as if we have a more important engagement? This is a problem. We cannot book God like an appointment. Do we see how off this is? It is putting restrictions on Him, but it is also not coming and saying, "God, what do You have in mind that You want to do today?" It certainly doesn't say, "God, how can we bless You? How can we love You?"

Are we saying you need to plan services to last all day? No. To be clear, there is nothing wrong with having a basic sense of service length. People should have a general sense of what to expect. (Parents need to plan if they need to feed their kids before they come or pack a snack.) However, there needs to be a willingness to blow up the model to stay in step with Him.

Practically speaking, we once had a Sunday morning service that literally went until sunrise the next morning. We sang, supernaturally, for over 20 hours at God's leading. That kind of thing is impossible. But, when we knew God had entered the room, we were not going to leave. We had someone order lunch for those who chose to stay. When we realized this was not going to end even as evening came, we had someone go get dinner for everyone. Then, when we realized this was going to go into the night, we had someone go get cots for the kids to sleep in the worship center. We do need to show hospitality to people, yes, but never at the cost of honoring God with hospitality.

When God wants to move, so often the response He gets from His Church is that it is impossible, forgetting He is the God of the impossible. We need a revolution that puts first things first, one that gives God more than a sliver on Sunday.

44. Have the Courage to Ask the Questions

Until we measure what matters, we will not reorient to what matters. If you do not measure what matters, your church will, by default, revert to defining success by what is easiest to measure. There is a better way, but we must have the courage to know the truth about whether or not disciples are in our pews.

Churches can take fifteen minutes once a year and have everyone present fill out an in-person survey, giving you such a high proportion of your potential respondents that your data will be very solid. Instead of asking people what they like and don't like, what makes them come or leave, find out about their love for God, their belief in what God says, and their faith demonstrated by obedience to what God says. If you aren't sure where to start or prefer to begin with something already created, we're happy to give access to the survey we use if that is helpful (which also will give you benchmarks against the aggregate of existing data from other churches).

To stay focused and accountable to the main things, we need to measure what God measures.

45. Stop Outsourcing Discipleship to the Government

Parents must be smarter disciple-makers and stop doing what everyone else is doing, which is obviously not working! Peers and other influencers appear to impact the worldview of teenagers even more than that of their parents (otherwise, generational differences would be much less than they are). Parents must overcome that strong influence with intentionality.

Most of us went to public school, and we think that we turned out fine; however, what used to be is not what is. The education system has moved far beyond teaching core subjects such as reading, writing, and arithmetic. Science is now firmly defined within the scope of naturalism, not permitting the most logical answers as answers if they come from outside of the naturalistic worldview.

The nation's education system has become the Sunday school program of the secular humanistic worldview. Sex education programs, once about abstinence or safety, have become trojan horses for the LGBTQ+ agenda to desensitize our kids to sexual immorality.

On top of what is sanctioned, students face pressures from their peers, unlike anything any generation has ever faced in America. Whereas previous generations were all tempted to drink, do drugs, or have sex, now Christian teenagers face overwhelming animosity. By simply being Christian, they are no longer just called and considered "prudes," but instead, they are referred to as haters, anti-science, and much, much more.

The discipleship of government schools is one of a godless ideology. We must be careful, be prayerful, be wise, and be Spirit-led. There are other educational options out there, each with unique upsides and downsides, and these should be considered seriously by parents. Are we saying all Christian parents should pull their kids out of public schools? No, but we are saying school selection should be a matter of much prayer, that parents must engage closely with what their kids are learning, and that parents should be aware of alternatives as they pray through each kid's path.

One of those alternative options is to homeschool. If you homeschool, the biggest upside is, of course, a completely controlled environment for your kid's education and development, but the downside is, of course, that it requires one spouse to be at home and unable to work. The fear of the unknown can be quite overwhelming for those not trained as educators. However, there is so much help out there. For example, there are video curriculum programs available that make the impossible very possible today. There are homeschool cohorts that exist at churches everywhere. Your kids can grow and develop relationships with other homeschooled kids, sharpening their relational skills, while also receiving great care. Additionally, the flexibility of homeschooling works wonders for pastors who work on weekends and evenings.

Another option is Christian school. This has long been considered a leading alternative, but many claim that the anecdotal results in terms of their kids' faith haven't lived up to their expectations. Just know that not all schools produce the same discipleship outcomes in terms of vitality or passion in pursuit of Christ. So, if you choose Christian school, be wise. You don't want to be one of those who fifteen years from now is blown away that you spent a hundred grand on primary education only to have an ex-Christian adult child. (This is very common!) No matter the path you choose, you cannot fully outsource your kids' discipleship.

If you do choose the Christian school path, you need to be aware that blending worldly ambition with Christianity in elite private schools often injects a generation with an inoculated version of Christianity that makes them more immune to the real thing. There are certain things Christianity does not blend well with—for example, a Christian country club. That is not going to be a baby that can be born without significant impact to the DNA of Christianity in it! Christianity does not have a hard time blending with education. However, there is a rub in trying to blend it with the form of an elite and expensive private education, which Christian education frequently becomes.

There are also various charter schools that are run by Christians depending on where you live. In these places, your kid won't get pulled in by counselors, asked their gender, and coached into full adherence to such a thing apart from your knowing. However, the peer influence will likely be the same or similar to the public school setting.

At the point of writing this, there is a lot of experimenting happening in this sphere, and it's possible things could change significantly by the time you read this. The bottom line is that there are other options available that may be better for your kids than the standard government schooling. However, if you stay the mainstream course with education, just know the truth. You are sending your kids into a full immersion of secular humanistic philosophy and ideology. Their peers' perspectives will impact them as much or more than their teachers, and as a result, your evenings and weekends must be filled with great spiritual intentionality. You cannot allow your calendars to be filled in the evenings and weekends by the school's extracurricular activities. Otherwise, you will have little to no time for making Christ the center of their lives.

To raise up a first-love revolution generation, we cannot keep outsourcing discipleship to the government's education programs and expect different results with our kids.

46. Put Pastors Back in the Prayer Closet

The apostles of the early Church raised up deacons to manage the affairs of the Church saying, "'But we will devote ourselves to prayer and to the ministry of the word'" (Acts 6:4). This statement sets the priority for what teachers and key leaders of each and every church should be doing.

Nothing is more important for the spiritual vitality of a church than the spiritual vitality of its leader(s), and their prayers carry a disproportionate impact on a church. We do not need more programs. We need more power. With little prayer, there is little power. With little prayer from those in positions of authority, there is little power on their lives.

Keep in mind that God does not anoint places or programs, but He does anoint people. When we recognize an anointing on a house (meaning, a church), that is, in truth, an anointing on the leaders of that church. When they go, it will go, unless those who follow them continue to seek God and depend on His grace. We cannot overstate the significance of the leaders and teachers being first in the place of prayer. It impacts everybody.

Anointing flows from the place of intimacy with God—from prayer, from pressing, and from purity. The lead pastor and consistent teaching pastors absolutely must devote at least two hours of their days to time in worship, in prayer, in personal study of the Word (not sermon prep), and in communion with the Lord in the secret place. If the church leaders around them cannot handle the other aspects of leading, pastoring, and managing the affairs of the church, then those leaders need to be replaced with others who are gifted and willing to do so. Also, where there is a solo pastor, deacons need to be raised up to do what the original deacons did, so that the pastor can devote himself or herself to prayer and to ministry of the Word.

Congregants, the lead pastor of the church is a shepherd to you, but he/she must be the type of shepherd who was prophesied to shepherd the New Testament churches: "'Then I will give you shepherds after My own heart, who will feed you on knowledge and understanding'" (Jeremiah 3:15).

Barna shares the following about the state of pastors today:

> "Other research among pastors I have undertaken suggests that pastor's jobs are overwhelming. The typical pastor is expected by church members to handle an enormous number and range of tasks. In such situations it must be easy to neglect the fundamentals in order to address tasks that seem more pressing and urgent. Unfortunately, after a prolonged period of such neglect, the foundations become weak and the person changes—in this case, not for the better."[1]

Providing insight from his other research, Barna said,

> "For instance, one-third of all pastors do not read the Bible during a typical week . . . That might be compared to a doctor not washing his hands before the operations he performs during a week; it's unthinkable, almost unimaginable . . . ."
>
> "Given that Bible reading is a major source of spiritual nourishment, no wonder so many pastors are spiritually weak and ineffective. Add to that

their frequent failure to pray, to connect with God through worship and thanksgiving, to spend time seeking God's direction and will, or regularly returning to Him to confess their sins and ask for forgiveness—it's no wonder so many pastors struggle."[2]

Pastors simply cannot devote themselves to prayer and the ministry of the Word while leading and managing everything and providing pastoral counseling to all in the congregation. In too many cases, the pastor of today has become the Moses of the Old Testament, of whom Jethro showed up and essentially said, "This is crazy! You cannot be meeting with everyone and deciding all these disputes! Raise up others to do that!"

So many pastors are nice people who do not want to say, "No." If a pastor does say, "No," please understand, and even better than that, make sure to make much of the grace of God that is flowing through your small group leader and/or serving team leaders. Your lead pastor and the teaching pastors should be primarily ministering to you by praying for you and feeding you with the teaching of the Word. It is not good to place other requirements on those people. Every time they say, "Yes," to one person, they simultaneously say, "No," to everyone else.

We cannot have a first-love revolution if the lead pastor and teaching pastors of a church are not leading the way in intimacy with the Lord and not leading the way in seeking the presence, power, and protection of the Lord in the place of prayer.

11

A Picture of a First-Love Revolution Church

What does a first-love revolution church look like in summary? It returns to its roots as a church of Word and Spirit, worship and prayer.

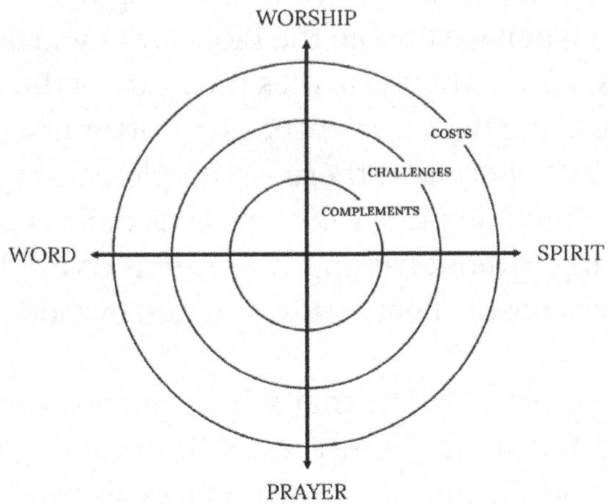

To explain the diagram above a little bit, with Word and Spirit, worship and prayer, at the point where there is only a little bit of each (represented by the innermost circle), this is where you will find complementary Christianity. Complementary Christianity is the "Jesus makes your life better" version of Christianity. It contains only a slight portion of the Word of God, a sprinkling of the Spirit, a small emphasis on Biblical worship, and a smattering of prayer.

Where you have a significant portion of all—or some—of these, you will find challenging Christianity (represented by the middle circle). This version of Christianity challenges you to take your next step, get better, and go a little further in Word or Spirit, worship or prayer.

At the outer perimeter is costly Christianity. When we uphold the full counsel of God's Word and expect Christians to live in obedience to all of the Lord's commands, it is beyond challenging. It is costly. It's the same thing with the Spirit—to seek and say, "Yes," to all of what the Spirit says and does is beyond challenging. It is costly. Likewise, when we uphold the Biblical standards of worship fully, it's costly. It crucifies the pride of the flesh. It's the same thing with prayer too. To scatter in a smattering of prayer here and there is complementary. To call people to include prayer in their lives daily is challenging. Praying without ceasing, however, is costly. Laboring in prayer is costly. Being truly directed by God in prayer is costly.

Think of first love as that which pushes to the outer perimeter of this picture, even desiring to go beyond the line, and the idolatry of attendance as the force that presses inward on this diagram. Otherwise stated, when first love is in place, you will find the church getting back to "all-all" Christianity (meaning pursuing all of all four of these), costly Christianity.

When we love God with all of us, teaching obedience to all of God's Word flows naturally. When we idolize attendance, we want to cut back on cost and loss while emphasizing benefit and blessing.

When we love God with all of us, being led by His Spirit and seeking His presence fully flows naturally. We say, "Yes," to all of who He is and all of what He wants to do. When we idolize attendance, we move what some find offensive, unbelievable, or uncomfortable to the back room, even if it's Him.

When we love God with all of us, we want to worship Him sacrificially. When we idolize the attendance of people, we shrink back from undignified expressions of love and affection for Him.

When we love God with all of us, dependence and desperation in the place of prayer make sense. We need Him. We want Him, and we want the knowledge of His glory to fill the earth. We are burdened for every testimony of His gravity and greatness to become known. When we idolize attendance, prayer gets puny, because we have what it takes to give the people what they want.

In our attempts at prevalence, we have lost power. There are accelerations of His Spirit at the intersections of these particular means of grace. Take note of almost any church body where the presence and power of God is at work, and you will find a house of Word *and* Spirit or one of worship *and* prayer. When all four are embraced fully and wholly, His grace flows more freely and abundantly.

Part III

Our Story

12

Same Race, New Roof

We planted Revolution Church in 2020 (originally named Church of the Front Range). However, our story didn't start there. Seven years earlier, I (Shane) became the lead pastor of a large Presbyterian church, and Rebekah joined the staff in 2014. Initially, we led the church according to the principles of the Church Growth Movement, and what happened? What you'd expect to happen. Remember the formula. Quality + Relevance – Cost = What? Attendance. Growing attendance is exactly what we saw.

However, beginning in 2016, we started to come under the convictions outlined in this book to lead the church in a different direction. Then, in May of 2017, Jon Tyson recommended that I (Shane) read some books on revival. (I actually did not know anything about past revivals, believe it or not.) I read a number of them, including *Why Revival Tarries* by Leonard Ravenhill. I felt very challenged by his statement, "[M]inisters who do not spend two hours a day in prayer are not worth a dime a dozen, degrees or no degrees."[1] As a megachurch preacher with so many responsibilities, I was somewhat shocked by his statement. I remember thinking, "He obviously doesn't know how busy I am." However, I decided to take him up on the prayer challenge!

What happened next should come as no surprise to anyone. After a week of praying two hours daily, I noticed my heart and mind were cleaner and less prone toward sin. Then a few days after that, I began to be more sensitive to the Spirit's presence and also more sensitive to the presence of demonic spirits. I didn't know what to make of it, but I recognized that all the time in prayer was unmistakably making a big difference.

From there, I was catalyzed into a life of intercession. Two weeks later, I was crying out for revival in tears and agony that I knew were supernatural, as if the heart of God was getting pressed through me in praying for a mighty move of His Spirit. During that time, God placed the call to seek Him for revival so firmly in my heart that nothing has ever been able to shake it out, no matter how hard the shaking (and there has been some hard shaking)!

God did the same in our senior-most pastoral team. We started meeting for daily intercession, burdened to seek God for an outpouring of His Spirit. God's call in 2 Chronicles 7:14 for the people of God to humble themselves, pray, repent of sin, and seek His face became a mandate on our lives. At that time, we prayerfully came to understand revival as a mass acceleration of the Kingdom of God—a time when the "out" come "in," the "in" come "up," and the "up" go "out" at an accelerated rate.

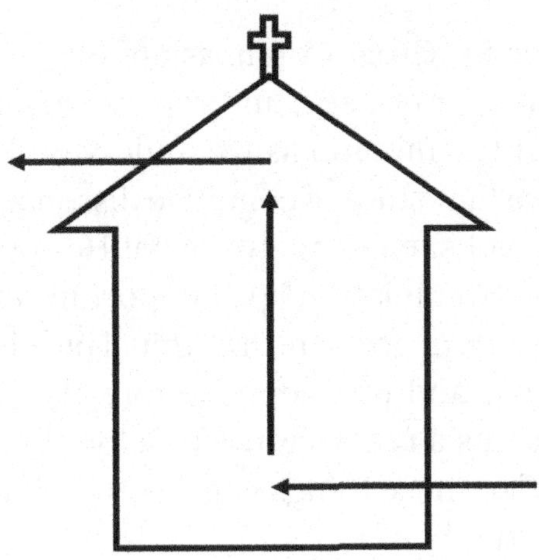

To be clear, Jesus is always doing these things. However, in revival, the rate at which the Kingdom of God advances is simply massively accelerated. Why? Because God pours out His Spirit, and where the King is, His Kingdom advances.

We understood the call on the people of God to humble themselves as a call to prayerful dependence and desperation. We also knew there was a strong correlation between seeking God's face and God's presence. (In Hebrew, these are the same word.) We knew there was a strong correlation between worship and seeking Him as well, and we understood that the call to repentance and the call to preach the full counsel of God's Word went hand in hand. All to say, in this call to revival, all these convictions around Word and Spirit, worship and prayer began to form.

What we did not understand, however, is how it all fit together. We were gripped to seek God for revival, but we also recognized that many of these things seemed to be costing us in "Great Commission" effectiveness. The call to humble, pray, seek, and repent seemed to negatively impact the mission as we understood it. I (Shane) lived in a constant state of cognitive dissonance, wanting to obey God but seeing much of what He commanded as costly to the "the mission." (It's important to know that with God, He often gives the individual puzzle pieces and looks for trust and obedience before He gives understanding.) It was a real wrestle for a lot of years to keep saying, "Yes," to these things while witnessing an adverse impact on attendance.

Nevertheless, along the way, by the grace of God, we found ourselves witnessing a mighty outpouring of the Holy Spirit. We'll never forget the way He changed the worship culture so dramatically in early 2018 or the way He began to heal people miraculously and instantly just a few months later! (Praise God, He has continued to do so since!) In 2019, God released a grace for hearing His voice which changed our church and granted the grace of prophecy to many in our midst. That same year, we witnessed Him save thousands. And, although 2020 was a hard year for everybody, He enabled us to write and teach messages six days a week. Only God!

There were so many miracles and only-God moments over those years; however, it was not all smooth sailing. Eventually, we ended up with two competing and incompatible churches trying to live under one roof, and one of those was no longer a good fit within the existing structures. In the middle of the COVID crisis of 2020, we left under extremely painful circumstances to plant Revolution Church, continuing to run this race under a new roof.

It was not until 2023 that God gave the key to understanding the exact nature of the revolution He was about to bring—a first-love revolution. When He did, it became clear that everything He had been telling us to do along the way perfectly fit with the true mission (Mark 12:30), just not our former understanding of the mission (Matthew 28:18-20).

When God revealed this, I (Shane) became overcome with conviction to the point I could not help but get on my face and weep on my office floor. He had been contending with my heart all this time. My own heart had been living in a divided place instead of loving Him with all. Following those tears, all of the internal tension—the feeling of being torn between doing what "works" and what God had been saying—was removed.

From that day forward, I've experienced profound freedom—as not one of God's commands and directives has ever been at even the slightest tension with the First and Greatest Commandment—to love the Lord my God with all my heart, all my soul, all my mind, and all my strength. Praise God! Furthermore, none of His commandments have been at odds with teaching others to do the same.

Here is what we want pastors to know about the journey to pursue a first-love revolution (which is worth reading for parishioners, too). The pain, loss, shame, dishonor, betrayal, rejection, and ridicule that we experienced were real and profound. There is no way around that. The journey is costly but worth it, because He is worth it and worthy of it. Let us not forget what Jesus said: "'If anyone wishes to come after Me, he must deny himself, and take up his cross and follow Me'" (Matthew 16:24).

Yet, it's not all cost. On the other side of a revolution that returns to its first love is the house of God filled with the presence of God and aligned to the will and ways of God. There is nothing greater than His presence, and the church that God has birthed out of this has been the greatest joy in ministry.

Can you imagine a church where almost everyone tithes and almost everyone serves? Can you imagine a church where your inbox isn't filled with the complaints most pastors receive but testimonies of what God has done? Can you imagine leading a church that prays around the clock, hears from the Lord, and believes in faith despite whatever hardships come? Can you imagine leading boldly and following the whispers of the Holy Spirit faithfully and being blessed as you do? Can you imagine preaching and knowing it's up to the Spirit, not you, to move people? Can you imagine gatherings where signs and wonders and testimonies of miracles are not only common but where the absence of them would be a cause for concern? With God, it is possible.

Can you imagine church becoming your favorite place, because His presence is manifest there? Can you imagine a gathering lasting for a couple of hours and not wanting to leave? Can you imagine the altars filled after you preach and not because of your skill as a motivational speaker? With God, it is possible.

Can you imagine speaking to a small room of people and, at the end, not walking away feeling like you are a loser, a failure, or incompetent? Can you imagine preaching and not having every empty chair become a statement about your success level? (Imagine walking away from preaching to a small crowd and feeling instead like you just hit a grand slam and won the World Series, because God's heart was moved! With God, it is possible. We can testify to it.) Can you imagine presenting the gospel every week and not fearing that none would raise their hand or come to the altar, because almost always with God's power present, He does it, and when He does, you take no credit but you feel a lot of joy?

You may be thinking, "None of that is possible." You are right. It is not possible in the natural. But, with God, all things are possible. Yet, getting there isn't easy. A revolution will expose the idols that sustain status quo—the idols of humanism, ambition, prestige, prominence, power, religiosity, self-righteousness, doubt, disbelief, and insecurity (that you would have never guessed were there in you and those around you). But, if you stay the course out of love for God, the church will be purified, and the Spirit will respond to the seeking of God's people.

And, mark our words, when you set out to lead a church whose aim is to love God with all of their heart, soul, mind, and strength, God is going to part seas and move mountains in your midst, just like He did for us. Within six weeks of launch, God gave us a closed-down Sweet Tomatoes restaurant to rent and provided the funds to purchase the audio/visual equipment as well as the materials and volunteer labor needed to renovate the entire thing. (This included demolition, building walls, carpeting, painting, stage building, and more!) Seriously, we launched within six weeks! God makes a way!

In only nine months of existence, God then made it possible to purchase a 50,000-square-foot facility whose debt service was less per month than renting a

10,000-square-foot former Sweet Tomatoes building! Only God!

Within one year of launching, God made it possible to bring all 20 staff (who willingly left their jobs and salaries) onto payroll and restore them to their previous salaries! Only God! (And He provided for each one of them in unique and miraculous ways while they went without a salary. Again, only God!)

Within another year, God made it possible to purchase a second facility in Colorado Springs and plant a second location! Only God!

More importantly, God built a church that is a joy to pastor. They are servants. They are grateful. They seek the Kingdom of God. They are full of faith. They are hopeful. They are loving. They are dependent on the Lord. They repent. They inquire of the Lord, wait for His answers, and are swiftly led by Him. They are sacrificial and have been a steadfast source of joy and encouragement every step of the way. We are deeply grateful for each of them.

Now, to be clear, things aren't perfect of course. We do have problems. People go off the rails. If you pursue the revolution, you will have problems too. However, a revolution church's orientation dramatically changes the experience of the church itself. A revolution church is aimed at moving the heart of God, not moving a room full of people. When this aim is rightly directed, the room of people becomes quite different, and the difference experienced as a pastor is monumental. We wish every pastor could experience it.

There is a place of freedom for both pastors and parishioners, where you can show up with a singular eye, which is an eye to love Him with all of you. You don't have to judge your church's success based on how many people come. Jesus doesn't. In truth, the revolution will lead you to receive greater commendation from our Lord on the day you stand before Him, while also setting you free from the tyranny of ungodly scorecards on this earth. Never forget, the ambition of the apostles who were sent by the Lord was never a bloated Bride, but a pure and spotless Bride. Be free and expect some birthing pains on the path toward freedom.

And remember, we cannot pass on what we do not possess. We all want to raise up a generation who will remain faithful to the end, no matter the cost and no matter the loss. Have we considered that enduring cost and loss ourselves may be the best way to prepare them to do that? We must be those who refuse to cut out cost, compromise, and concession in order to avoid loss ourselves if we are going to pass along an enduring faith to them.

How can we pass along persevering faith if we abandon the courses God calls us to and the promises He speaks over us when we face setbacks, opposition, and delays? We can't. How can we raise up a Joshua and Caleb generation if we are not Joshuas and Calebs? We can't. How can we raise up a generation willing to sacrifice when there is no choice, if we did not sacrifice when there was a choice? We can't. If we turn around when we see giants and walls, we are not Joshuas or Calebs, and we cannot pass along what we do not possess.

We don't wish pain and cost on any of you, but if you do pay a price and remain faithful, the next generation will benefit from your testimony greatly. The next generation needs to grow up hearing these testimonies—testimonies of persevering in faith to do what God had called, testimonies of enduring persecution, setback, delay, and cost but remaining steadfast and seeing God's faithfulness to do as He promised with those who persevered.

As you seek God's face and wait on His faithfulness, you do not have to carry that feeling of waiting until then—until the day revival comes—to fulfill the mission. Today, this day, even if filled with every obstacle and hurdle to growing the church, is a day we can love Him with all of us and teach others to do the same. We're not waiting to win; we're winning as we wait. (Our hearts burn for every pastor and parishioner reading this to feel the same!)

We hope you are praying for a mighty outpouring of God's Spirit that revives the Church in your region as we are. As you do, remember that what people are born into, they reproduce. As more are swept into the household of faith, where Mark 12:30 is the mission, and as more live the mission with every decision, they will teach others to do the same.

Part IV

Q&A

13

But What About?

If you're going on this journey, you will face some pushback and opposition along the way. Included in this chapter are some of the things you'll hear people say and some ways we have found helpful to navigate those responses. You may want to simply look over the headings for this section of the book in the "Table of Contents" and read those that catch your attention or are particularly relevant at the time. However, if you do skip this section, be sure to read the chapter titled, "A Final Word," before you put this on the shelf!

? God Is Sovereign, So Why All the Emphasis on Seeking?

One of the things you'll likely hear is, "Why all the intensity and emphasis on seeking? If God is going to do something, isn't He going to do it no matter what we do? Isn't that what it means for God to be sovereign?" There is a lot to unpack in these unbiblical statements. So much of our theology does not come from the Bible but rather from traditions taught by men.

First, God doing what He is going to do regardless of what we do is not what it means for God to be sovereign. We've got to know the Word of God and hold to what it says. Is God, God? Yes. Does God have and reserve the right to do whatever He wants (consistent with His character), whenever He wants? Yes. Can He and does He act independently of us? Yes. Are there times that He makes an oath and swears that what He has ordained will surely come to pass (despite what we do or do not do)? Yes. But is all of that (or any of that) inconsistent with God saying, "If you do X, then I will do Y," something we see throughout Scripture? No. God's sovereignty is neither unresponsive nor indifferent. Sovereignty, human responsibility, and God's responsiveness to our actions are not incompatible.

On many occasions, God makes known an if/then possibility, and its fulfillment is only realized if one meets the stipulations that God has set. Furthermore, throughout Scripture, we see that the promises of God require participation. God has not changed. We once cataloged all the if/then statements of the New Testament. There are too many to put here, but here is an extremely truncated list.

In John 7:37–38, Jesus said, "'If anyone is thirsty, let him come to Me and drink. He who believes in Me, as the Scripture said, 'From his innermost being will flow rivers of living water.'" Who received this living water? Everyone? No, only those who came to Him. The promises of God require participation.

In Acts, God spoke through Peter:

"Repent, and each of you be baptized in the name of Jesus Christ for the forgiveness of your sins; and you will receive the gift of the Holy Spirit. For the promise is for you and your children and for all who are far off, as many as the Lord our God will call to Himself" (Acts 2:38-39).

Was everyone forgiven? Did every person receive the Holy Spirit? No, only those who repented. The promises of God require participation.

In Hebrews 3:6, we are told, "But Christ was *faithful* as a Son over His house—whose house we are, if we hold fast our confidence and the boast of our hope firm until the end." Are we part of Christ's house no matter what? No. This is true only if we hold fast until the end.

Again, God is sovereign, but what we do matters. Our God is a God who responds. Consider these verses as well:

- "'[I]f you forgive others for their transgressions, your heavenly Father will also forgive you'" (Matthew 6:14).
- "'[S]eek His kingdom, and these things will be added to you'" (Luke 12:31).
- "'If you abide in Me, and My words abide in you, ask whatever you wish, and it will be done for you'" (John 15:7).
- "'[T]he one who endures to the end, he will be saved'" (Matthew 24:13).
- "God causes all things to work together for good to those who love God" (Romans 8:28).
- "'By your standard of measure it will be measured to you; and more will be given you besides'" (Mark 4:24).
- "Humble yourselves in the presence of the Lord, and He will exalt you" (James 4:10).
- "Draw near to God and He will draw near to you" (James 4:8).

- "'[W]hoever loses his life for My sake and the gospel's will save it'" (Mark 8:35).
- "'He who receives a prophet in *the* name of a prophet shall receive a prophet's reward'" (Matthew 10:41).
- "'Therefore repent and return, so that your sins may be wiped away, in order that times of refreshing may come from the presence of the Lord'" (Acts 3:19).
- "'[I]f anyone hears My voice and opens the door, I will come in to him and will dine with him, and he with Me'" (Revelation 3:20).

What are other examples of if/then statements in Scripture?

"[W]hen you pray, go into your inner room, close your door and pray to your Father who is in secret, and your Father who sees *what is done* in secret will reward you" (Matthew 6:6).

[O]ne who looks intently at the perfect law, the *law* of liberty, and abides by it, not having become a forgetful hearer but an effectual doer, this man will be blessed in what he does (James 1:25).

"Whoever then annuls one of the least of these commandments, and teaches others *to do* the same, shall be called least in the kingdom of heaven; but whoever keeps and teaches *them*, he shall be called great in the kingdom of heaven" (Matthew 5:19).

"[A]sk, and it will be given to you; seek, and you will find; knock, and it will be opened to you. For everyone who asks, receives; and he who seeks, finds; and to him who knocks, it will be opened" (Luke 11:9–10).

"[I]f you have faith and do not doubt, you will not only do what was done to the fig tree, but even if you say to this mountain, 'Be taken up and cast into the sea,' it will happen" (Matthew 21:21).

[I]f any of you lacks wisdom, let him ask of God, who gives to all generously and without reproach, and it will be given to him. But he must ask in faith without any doubting (James 1:5-6).

[W]hatever a man sows, this he will also reap. For the one who sows to his own flesh will from the flesh reap corruption, but the one who sows to the Spirit will from the Spirit reap eternal life (Galatians 6:7–8).

"[E]veryone who has left houses or brothers or sisters or father or mother or children or farms for My name's sake, will receive many times as much, and will inherit eternal life" (Matthew 19:29).

[I]n everything by prayer and supplication with thanksgiving let your requests be made known to God. And the peace of God, which surpasses all comprehension, will guard your hearts and your minds in Christ Jesus (Philippians 4:6–7).

As you can see, there are many if/then realities laid out by God in Scripture, and truly there are so many more!

Teachings that diminish or discount the if/then realities of Scripture lack biblical fidelity. The promises of God require participation. God is sovereign, but God's sovereignty doesn't make our seeking insignificant. God could not be more clear in His Word that what we do matters and that He responds to our seeking: "'You will seek Me and find *Me* when you search for Me with all your heart'" (Jeremiah 29:13).

In addition, we should recognize that even when God gives an oath, an unconditional promise, even that unconditional promise is just the floor, not the ceiling! At the very last gathering we had before the COVID lockdowns began (at the time, we did not know it would be our last gathering), I (Shane) was lying face down at the altar, praying for revival, and God met me in a powerful way. I won't disclose the details of that encounter here, but at that time, what He had promised conditionally before regarding revival, He covenanted to do.

That oath, that guarantee, however, could have brought about complacency, don't you think? I could have walked away saying, "I no longer have a need to pray. God swore it. He will do it. He guaranteed it, and He will carry me to it. I mean what is there to do now but to sit back and relax?" What a mistake that would have been, and what a mistake that would be for any of us! God's oaths and promises are not ceilings. They are floors. So, I did not stop seeking after the Lord. I thought to myself, "Revival is coming, and seeing it is good. Praise God! But, I am seeking God for far more than simply that!"

Be discerning. People have concocted theology after theology to say, in one way or another, that what we do doesn't matter. Itching ears long to hear this, because it alleviates a sense of responsibility. But this is an illusion born of a delusion, and when we stand before God, we will be judged according to His truth, the only truth, and not man's rendition of it.

Many want to be spiritually lazy and prioritize their lives around their own comforts, plans, and priorities and hear that it's inconsequential. So, when they start hearing of such striving, laboring, hungering, thirsting, and running after God and the Kingdom of God, they take aim at this truth, because they want to feel justified in their choices.

Do not be distracted or deterred. Discern what is going on and stay focused on bringing the Lord what He deserves, a church body in white-hot pursuit of Him.

? Aren't You Turning God into a Cosmic Vending Machine?

The whole concept that God responds to us (and that something we do could have anything to do with what God does) is going to be very countercultural to a Church that has been catering to itching ears for years. Why? Because if this is true, we can no longer be comfortable in complacency, indifference, apathy, or inaction. As you pursue the first-love revolution, you may hear people say, "You're treating God like a vending machine and teaching others to do the same." Is that true?

To acknowledge that God responds as He promises is not dishonoring Him but the opposite is. As we seek God, we believe He rewards, but we also don't get to specify how, when, or where He rewards either. For those who think they can use God to get what they want, they can't.

Yes, we seek God in faith that He always rewards when we earnestly seek Him; however, we don't know the exact way or when His reward will come.

Sometimes, the reward may even be something we would not necessarily count as a reward immediately. If you've ever gone through pressing and refinement, you will understand this. As you seek Him, He exposes what is within, and that leads you to cry out to Him. When you cry out to Him, He answers, and as a result, you experience more of Him. The process of pressing and refinement is a reward even if it does not feel like it immediately. If we quit seeking when God does not come through or at least not on our timeline or in our prescribed way, it only reveals we were not seeking out of love for Him but love for ourselves.

God is the One who says He rewards. To believe what He says, to honor what He says, is not to treat Him as a vending machine unless you come to Him with specific demands. Those who love God pursue God, and as they run after Him, they simply say, "I love You. I need You. I want You. I want more of You, and I do not demand of You what I think that should look like. God, You know best. Have Your way. If it's being refined by the fire, 'Yes!' If it is learning how to take up my cross every day, 'Yes!' If it is hearing more of Your voice and being told what to do more often, even told things I don't want to do, 'Yes!' If it is an encounter with Your power, which is quite frightening, 'Yes!' If it is a vision that leaves me feeling weak, sick, and incapacitated like Daniel, 'Yes!' I do not demand what or how, but I believe in seeking You, You will permit me to find more of You. As long as it's You, God, I want You! God, I do have specific asks, but I am not going to be one who quits if I don't get what I have specifically asked for."

? What about Grace?

Others might say to you, "What about grace? You are making everything about works!"

What is the nature of grace? Grace is undeserved. Mercy is the same. Everything we receive from God is mercy and grace. Knowing that, we have often jettisoned the passages in which God is extremely plainspoken about rewarding our actions, because we assume these two concepts are incompatible. God, however, does not contradict Himself. When two things in Scripture are seemingly at odds, it's not our job to dismiss what we think doesn't fit. It's our job to humbly come to God and ask Him to show us how they reconcile. Let's do that now.

In Luke 17, Jesus tells a parable of a master and a slave, representative of God and us, and closes it by saying,

> "He does not thank the slave because he did the things which were commanded, does he? So you too, when you do all the things which are commanded you, say, 'We are unworthy slaves; we have done *only* that which we ought to have done'" (Luke 17:9–10).

Jesus is clear. When we give God what He is due, that does not make us deserving of something from God. Jesus' teaching underscores the point that whatever we receive from God is mercy and grace. At the same time, God says, "And without faith it is impossible to please *Him*, for he who comes to God must believe that He is and *that* He is a rewarder of those who seek Him" (Hebrews 11:6). Which is true? Both! We don't deserve, but God rewards us.

How do these two concepts come together? Here's how. A reward can be grace. Grace is not inherently anti-reward. Reward is not inherently anti-grace. For example, we can reward our kids for things they do without them thinking that, if they do those things, they are entitled to that reward. You can reward in grace. That's what God does.

To be very clear, on account of our actions, do we earn the grace of God in whatever form His grace is returned? No. That would be to see and treat the grace of God as a wage. (A wage is issued as payment; a reward is given in recognition.) God's grace returned is not a wage, but a reward, which is the result of His faithfulness (i.e., His commitment to recognize what He has said He will), not our deservingness. This is why we discourage using the phrase "purchased in the place of prayer." We cannot buy anything and do not deserve anything from God. It's all mercy and grace.

On February 8, 2023, God made His presence manifest at our Wednesday night gathering in one of the most palpable ways our church body had ever encountered. I (Rebekah) was literally floored, along with many others who were there. I still find it hard to put into words what I experienced of His presence that night. The best way I can describe it is that the King entered the room. His presence was majestic—His love and His goodness, along with His power and His holiness filled the room. In a moment, surrounded by people who were on their faces before the Lord, I felt a head truth supernaturally pressed deep into my heart by the Spirit—we were not entitled to His presence on account of our seeking, and yet our seeking was not insignificant.

Those who love God desire to please Him, and so they do believe He is as responsive as He reveals Himself to be in His Word. When God does reward us, it is not a statement about us (what we did), but a statement about His faithfulness (to do what He said He would do, even though we do not and cannot deserve it).

? If God Shows Up, Won't Everyone Show Up?

You'll hear this and forms of this again and again: "If God is present and moving, wouldn't everyone recognize it? Wouldn't they come running to the place to be part of it?" The underlying unspoken truth would often be better said, "If my friends or family members don't like it, it's obviously not of God."

Will everyone recognize God's presence and activity and want to be a part of it? Would those who identify with Him and even some believers ever actually prefer His absence? What does the Bible say? The best answer to these questions comes from reading the Gospels. Jesus, God in the flesh, was walking among men, preaching in the power of God to men, working the mighty works of God in front of men, and even raising the dead. But, the vast majority rejected Him. If God is present and moving, will everyone recognize His presence and flock to Him? The simple answer is, "No." That has been true historically, and sadly, it remains true today.

In addition, if you have not been in the midst of a mighty move of the Spirit yet, it's hard to imagine that believers—or anyone present for that matter—could fail to recognize it. But those who have been in the midst of a move can tell you that God can be moving powerfully in the room, and it not be experienced by all. Why? We all do have equal access to God through Christ Jesus but not all access equally. Seeking matters.

Don't forget that in Acts 2, God moved as unmistakably as anyone could imagine. Yet, all did not recognize God's activity. Some did, but Acts 2:13 tells us, "But others were mocking and saying, 'They are full of sweet wine.'" Who mocked? Was it only the Romans and not any of the Jews? No. People who assumed they were "in" and believed they were "in" missed it, just like they did with Jesus.

The inconsistency of some encountering God's presence, while others do not, can then further prick and provoke self-righteousness and insecurity in a major way. People will ask, "Why them? Why not me?" From that place, they can either get hungry for more of God, or they can self-justify by denying, rejecting, or attacking the move of the Spirit in their midst.

We've seen this play out firsthand. For example, there was a period of time, when we first said, "Yes," to God's invitation to bring Him a 24/7 continual assembly of perpetual praise, that we started experiencing God's work through some unusual signs and wonders, primarily during those 24/7 times in the worship center, outside of the normal church gatherings. Some of those signs and wonders were easier to accept as Biblically supernatural (such as seeing lights in the room, experiencing gusts of wind, and smelling supernatural smells of incense). But, there were also some things that were very hard for some people to accept (glitter appearing where it wasn't, sand being left behind after people got up from prayer at the altar, feathers showing up where they were not before, people hearing musical instruments audibly and supernaturally when they were not playing in the room but were accompanying whoever was leading the 24/7 worship, various colors of what appeared to be gemstones appearing, raindrops falling in the worship center when it wasn't raining outside, an actual pillar of cloud/smoke, etc.).

Desiring to honor what God was doing, we, of course, permitted people to testify about what they saw and heard, and as they did, they testified not just to the sign itself, but the meaning of it and how God impacted them through it. However, as they did, we began to get a handful of people protesting these testimonies, because, they said, some of the signs and wonders were not things found in the Bible. As a result, we delivered a message on July 23, 2023, to address how we evaluate a sign or wonder along Biblical lines. In short, the question, "Is it Biblical?" should not be equated with, "Has God done this exact thing before?" Rather, "Is it Biblical?" should mean, "Is it consistent with the character of God and His will and ways as revealed in Scripture?" He is the God of the new thing, and by definition, a new thing is, in fact, new.

When God started to do these unique signs and wonders, we were discussing all that was happening with an out-of-state lawyer (who now is the General Counsel for our church). He said something insightful: "People accuse God of not speaking or making Himself known, but then when He does, they want to dictate how. Like 'God, I want You to move in a way, speak in a way that is uniquely supernatural, intellectually satisfying, and sufficiently dignified.' He is accused if He does and accused if He doesn't." He also said, "It's broken logic to suggest that God is doing something but that attention shouldn't be drawn to it. Either you don't believe He did it, or if you do, then by virtue of God's acting, God is drawing attention to Himself and what He is doing (actions always draw attention). Who are you to say we should not give attention to what God is acting to draw attention to?" We could not have agreed more. Yet, some people left during this incredible season of God's activity. They did not recognize God at work, and they would not accept these supernatural occurrences as being anything other than distractions.

How did we prayerfully interpret and handle these occurrences? In Luke 19:17, Jesus said, "'Well done, good slave, because you have been faithful in a very little thing, you are to be in authority over ten cities.'" The word for "little thing" is actually the word meaning least, not little.

Pay attention, because when God first begins to move, He may test you with the "least" to see if you'll be faithful before He entrusts you with much. When you're entrusted with the least, you will know because honoring that which is least will seem to come with more cost than burying that which is least. You will only be faithful with the least when you simply want to love and honor the One who entrusted it to you no matter the cost to yourself, because honoring and stewarding the least will feel more costly than beneficial. That is precisely the reason stewarding the least qualifies you to be entrusted with much (because only those who put loving Him first will honor the least, and only those who put loving Him first can be entrusted with much).

Certainly, some will reject the "least" things of God. But, don't be mistaken, even the greatest revivals in all of history from Acts 2 to the present have been opposed and rejected by many Christians. The spirit of doubt and disbelief resides in many, and the spirit of religion, self-righteousness, and pride cannot handle God moving mightily among others or in someone else, if not also in them. For others, they will not embrace the cost and loss of what others think. As Jesus said in John 5:44, "'How can you believe, when you receive glory from one another and you do not seek the glory that is from the *one and* only God?'"

It's worth disclosing that it was immediately after preaching that message on these "offensive" signs and wonders on Sunday, July 23, 2023, that God gave this message about a first-love revolution that you're reading now. It truly felt like a clear commendation from the Lord, "You were faithful with the least, now I will entrust more to you."

So in summary, if God is present, will everyone flock? No. Certainly, there are times when God is moving so mightily that more come than leave, but that is not always the case. We want to be those who are faithful to keep saying, "Yes," to Him whether it leads to more or fewer people present.

When God first called us into 24/7, I (Rebekah) was struck with how few were at the manger when Christ arrived, and how God longs to find those who will care for what He has conceived in His Spirit while it is in its infancy. God looks for Marys and Josephs who will steward and not despise small beginnings—who, out of love for Him, will care for His new thing before the benefit of it appears to outweigh the cost of it.

Why does God often bring things into the world in the form of a seed, a baby, a small beginning? Because, He is wise. We often think, "God, the new thing that You are doing, You should begin with a bang and broadcast broadly." Instead, often the new things He is doing are relatively unknown, because the initial size and scale sift out those who want to serve Him for Him from those who want to use Him for them.

We often fail to recognize and honor the seed form of what God is doing. However, the enemy is not as undiscerning of God's purposes as we often are. The spirit of Herod (which was a spirit of insecurity) always sees and goes after the new thing conceived of the Spirit while it is small and fragile in its infancy. So, don't despise small beginnings (as few are willing to be Marys or Josephs), but don't be surprised when small beginnings are contested either (because the enemy recognizes what that baby will become).

? Can We Really Move God's Heart?

Two similar questions that you will hear are, "Isn't it prideful to believe that God's heart can be moved?" and, "Isn't it impossible to move God's heart since He is impassable and immutable?" The most straightforward reading of Scripture, both what God declares and demonstrates, is that He is responsive and that His heart can be moved. Believing what God says is not prideful. Disbelieving what God says is.

Did not Abraham's faith move the heart of God? When Abraham did not withhold his own son, but retained his faith that the promise would come through Isaac despite taking him up Mt. Moriah as a sacrifice, that moved God's heart and secured Abraham as the father of faith to all who have faith!

Did not Noah's obedience move the heart of God? When Noah obeyed despite the unbelievability of a global flood and the sheer enormity of the impossibility of such a task, he became the ancestor of all who would follow thereafter, the new Adam of the new world!

Was God not moved by Caleb's unwavering confidence in the face of the giants and walls? Was God unmoved by Caleb's correction of those who spoke otherwise, even when he and Joshua stood alone as two of only two million? God was moved, and so much so that Caleb was preserved to possess the promise!

Was God not moved with Phinehas' zeal? When sin entered the camp, and he took up the spear, did God not promise him an everlasting priesthood because of it?

What about the alabaster jar broken on Jesus? Was the heart of God moved by the one? She was grafted into the telling of the gospel forever for it!

We serve a God who is no less moved by the lavish love, costly sacrifice, or unwavering confidence in Him than any loving parent of a child today. We serve a God whose eyes are ranging to and fro throughout the earth for one whose heart is fully His (2 Chronicles 16:9). He is moved by such a one and shows Himself strong through them. We serve a wildly responsive God! Seek Him, and you will see! He will reward. You will encounter Him, hear from Him, receive keys never passed out before, hear inexpressible things, receive promises, get invited into grand purposes, and so much more! Faith believes this—that God rewards those who earnestly seek Him (Hebrews 11:6). So, believe it! It is true. (Such activities will also bring persecution. Rejoice for that too, because you get a great reward in Heaven for that as well!)

Now, some will object saying that God does not change. Is that true? Yes, it is. But, in what way? God's character does not change, but that does mean that God always does the same thing. He is a responsive God. That does not change who He is! Think of a child falling and scraping his knee. His mom picks him up, cleans the wound, and comforts him. Did she respond? Yes. Did her response change who she was? No. This is like that. God's character does not change. He is always just, always merciful, always true, always faithful, always gracious, always loving, and always present. He is who He is. He does not change, but that does not mean He always does the same thing in all situations.

When Nineveh repented, God relented. Similarly, in the book of Jeremiah, God declared,

> "At one moment I might speak concerning a nation or concerning a kingdom to uproot, to pull down, or to destroy *it*; if that nation against which I have spoken turns from its evil, I will relent concerning the calamity I planned to bring on it. Or at another moment I might speak concerning a nation or concerning a kingdom to build up or to plant *it*; if it does evil in My sight by not obeying My voice, then I will think better of the good with which I had promised to bless it" (Jeremiah 18:7–10).

God's character is consistent, and because of that, He responds differently to different situations. God doesn't always do the same, yet God does not change. His character doesn't change even when what He does changes. How is this possible? Because the same quality has a different expression depending on the circumstance. A dad who loves his son will behave very differently when bringing him home from the hospital than when disciplining him for doing something dangerous. However, in both instances, the loving father has not changed. In reality, some people's definition of immutability makes God quite mutable and quite inconsistent at a character level. Think about it. If you do the same thing no matter what the circumstance is, your character is constantly changing, inconsistent, and very mutable.

Furthermore, it goes without saying that if someone is portraying God as if He has no heartfelt response to what we do or the lack thereof, it's wildly inconsistent with Scripture. God is described as being provoked to anger (Deuteronomy 32:16), having regret (Genesis 6:6), being grieved (Ephesians 4:30), laughing (Psalm 2:4), being moved with compassion (Matthew 20:34), being provoked to jealousy (1 Kings 14:22) and more. Many of the verses reflecting these emotional responses in God are stated in such a way that it is clear that He was moved and provoked to such a response. If we claim the truth that "God never changes" means that He does not change in heart or action in response to what we do, then we are not protecting His unchangeable character, but rather portraying it as constantly changing. Never underestimate how much the heart of the Father is moved by even one of His children!

? Is This a Call to Small?

Some will respond to the first-love revolution, with its emphasis on God getting what He wants at the gathering, with a statement like, "So, long services and low attendance are the key to experiencing God's manifest presence?"

First of all, this question is offensive in its portrayal of God. God is not some machine that responds to levers, as if our formulaic approach to Him controls what He does.

Second, the first-love revolution is not a call to small. It is a call to cost. Will higher cost often result in fewer people being willing to pay it? In the American culture, as it stands today (although we are praying for that to change), the answer will often be, "Yes." However, we have observed in other countries that the same kind of costly Christianity receives a different response. In those settings, we've experienced services so long it would even make the pentecostals tired in America, and yet, witnessed thousands upon thousands of people showing up and sitting on the ground shoulder to shoulder for multiple hours. There are places where the soil is softer, even though they are often known as being "hostile" to the gospel.

Why is there that kind of response there and not here? The simple answer is that the people there are more desperate. They do not have so many lower and lesser things to fill them up; they are not entertaining themselves to death. God is perceived rightly to be the best there is. In summary, we're not claiming that a first-love revolution will always lead to smaller, but in certain cultures and conditions, it certainly might.

But, back to long gatherings or services, when you have the heart of the first-love revolution in place, you will often find longer, rather than shorter, gatherings. Is that because there is something significant in and of itself about a long service? No. A long service can be just as dead as a short one, and a long one absent of His presence is an even worse testimony than a short one absent of His presence! Yet, the reality is, in the midst of a first-love revolution, you will often find longer gatherings. Why is that? It's because we're waiting for the King to come, and we don't want to leave when He does.

What clears the way for the King to come? There is a lot wrapped up in this, but there are certain conditions that are conducive to His presence. When we have unrepentant sin, it creates barriers and blockades in place of a clear path. Is it possible for people to come in with soft, repentant hearts that have already confessed their sin and set their desire on seeking Him? Yes, but it does not happen without intentionality. Instead, what often happens as we begin to worship is that we become increasingly aware of our sinfulness, we repent, the blockades are removed, and then the path is finally created for the King to come in. That's when we experience His manifest presence. Sometimes we think we are waiting on God when He is really waiting on us!

Until we understand the holiness of God again, we will not comprehend this. If you want to reverse the direction of the analogy, Scripture plainly tells us who can ascend the hill of the Lord (Psalm 24:3–4) and who can dwell on God's holy mountain (Psalm 15). What are the requirements? Clean hands, pure hearts, and one whose speech, action, and heart are pure before Him.

Holiness, however, is not the only condition conducive for the coming of the King. There is also a heart that is willing to wait on God, that says He is the prize, and that loves Him so much it won't leave without being in His presence. A heart filled with this kind of love for God believes every moment of waiting, every minute of waiting, and every hour of waiting is nothing in comparison to His presence. There is a hunger and a thirst. There is a love and a desire. There is a seeking and a waiting that creates a place for the King to come. Those with this kind of love for God could not stand the thought of going home before the One who called the gathering had arrived.

Holiness and hunger prepare the way for the King to come. What else? God tells us there are two unique places and conditions in which He dwells. One, of course, is where two or three are gathered in His name (Matthew 18:20). According to Psalm 22:3, the other is in the praises of His people. (Psalm 22:3 is often translated as "enthroned in the praises," but the Hebrew is literally, "dwells in the praises.")

What does that tell us? When praise ceases and then starts, we should not expect that God's manifest presence has remained; when the gathering ceases and then starts, we should not expect that He has remained. God only promises to dwell (not visit) in those two conditions. Therefore, when we gather back together seven days later and begin to praise again seven days later, we're not starting from where we left off. We are rebuilding a place for Him to dwell in that moment.

In summary, love waits; love waits for God. (It is worth testifying that since God has led us into a continual assembly of perpetual praise, there has been a palpable difference in His sustained manifest presence.)

? What about the Lost?

Those committed to the revolution that returns the Church to her first love will likely also hear, "But, what about the lost? Doesn't God want us to reach the lost?" Yes! He does, and yet, our attempts to improve upon God do not work, even when we suspect they do.

Back to our journey. In 2019, God had led us about as far away from the seeker-sensitive philosophy that I (Shane) had been trained in as possible, so much so that one of my seeker-sensitive, long-term buddies tried to stage an intervention to get me to turn away from this off-putting path! It was ironic, however, because during that time, we had just seen God save more people in a few weekends than what we had seen in the entire previous year!

It was clear that what God was doing was blowing up the seeker-sensitive wineskin and confounding people's minds. As part of that, we had been running a seeker-sensitive evangelistic program for years. We spent a lot of money running that program, but in truth, there were a relatively small number of salvations coming out of it. Everyone raved like it was the end-all-be-all, but we were seeing far more salvations per weekend in our old-school preaching and teaching than that seeker-sensitive program would see in a full year! Yet, some in the program, committed to the philosophy and methodology of the program, would attack the leaders of the church for not being more sensitive to the lost—regardless of the fruit.

If we have eyes to see, what does that show? It shows they thought the lost would be led to Christ through their particular model, approach, and rebrand of Christ and Christianity more so than God's unfiltered truth, power, and presence. Even when they witnessed God do the opposite of their indoctrinated philosophy, they still rejected it. They were more committed to rebranding Christianity in order to be seen and embraced by the world as palatable and rational than actually seeing the lost enter into eternity.

In a year of being led away from our former seeker-sensitive approach toward something that sounded as old as the sermons in the book of Acts themselves, we witnessed more salvations than ever before. From March 2019 to March 2020, we witnessed over 6,000 salvations! To put that in context, when I (Shane) was at a 20,000-per-weekend person church prior, the "Big Hairy Audacious Goal" (BHAG)[1] of our evangelism department was to see a Pentecost year where 2,000 people were saved in one year. That was truly a BHAG, but sadly, it never happened. However, in 12 months, we witnessed first-hand what prophetic preaching and powerful presence can do in comparison with man's best skills, strategies, smarts, and schemes. There is no comparison.

We wish for every church to see scores of salvations year after year and for those who are, praise the Lord! The point here is that the seeker-sensitive philosophy and methodology is overly assumed to "work." But, is it working, really? *The American Worldview Inventory 2021-22* reveals that:

Just 44% [of self-identified born-again Christians] believe that when they die they will go to Heaven, but only because they have confessed their sins and accepted Jesus Christ as their savior. In other words, nearly six out of 10 people who claim to be born-again do not meet the widely accepted, biblical definition of born-again[2] (aside added).

We need to realize that even where the data seems to show the seeker-sensitive model is working, a decision that doesn't trust in Christ's atoning work alone and a decision that never results in obedience to all that the Lord commands is no salvation decision at all. In that case, not a single disciple has been made. If anything, it has produced someone who has been inoculated to the true thing by the false assurance of a weakened strand of the living hope.

Every pastor needs to ask the Lord, "What percent of this church is truly saved?" Someone's presence at a service does not guarantee his/her presence in eternity. Jesus warned us,

"Enter through the narrow gate; for the gate is wide and the way is broad that leads to destruction, and there are many who enter through it. For the gate is small and the way is narrow that leads to life, and there are few who find it" (Matthew 7:13-14).

God loves the lost and cares about each one more than we can fathom. However, if you think you can improve upon the Spirit-filled preaching and call to repentance we find in the Scriptures to reach them, you are badly mistaken. Stop rebranding the Bible. Stop rebranding God. Stop rebranding Jesus. Let the lion of Judah be unveiled and the Spirit of Pentecost unleashed, and you'll see the dead come to life over and over again.

A first-love revolution believes the power and presence of God is what opens the eyes of the blind to turn from darkness to light and from the kingdom of darkness to that of the living God. What was the apostolic prayer for the Church regarding unbelievers visiting a church? "[T]he secrets of his heart are disclosed; and so he will fall on his face and worship God, declaring that God is certainly among you" (1 Corinthians 14:25). This is God's definition of a seeker-sensitive service! How far we've strayed from Scripture. Can you imagine? It can happen, but it takes a gathering where the King who called the meeting is present and the Spirit of the living God is moving mightily.

Does that mean we should not do anything to intentionally reach the lost? Of course not. We still should cast a broad net. With every single message, the gospel should be preached, and we should call for a response. We are to invite people always. But, to alter the aim of a gathering to make it more comfortable for the lost is unacceptable.

Every time we gather, we should imagine God on His throne and us gathering around Him. The fact that someone is present who doesn't know Him doesn't change the purpose and focus of the gathering. It's still His and for Him. For years, we have had some arguing that the Church should be oriented down, toward believers, while others have been arguing that the Church should be oriented out, toward unbelievers. The purpose of the Church is neither of these, but it is to be oriented up, toward God. So often, those who brought their guests want others to tone down their worship, their celebration of the King, and want the King's heralds to soften the message to make it more palatable. Is that right? No. It is not right. We do not minimize God one millimeter to be more pleasing to the pride-filled flesh of fallen man.

And, let's be honest. A lost person is not just a "guest." A lost person is loved by God, yes, but is also an enemy of God at enmity with God (Romans 5:10; Colossians 1:21)! Can you imagine telling those who celebrate a king to calm it down a bit, because one of his enemies is there, and it is off-putting to them? It's ludicrous and much repentance is needed for making God *a* priority in His own house versus *the* priority.

And why, by the way, do we think that enthusiasm for God that falls short of the world's enthusiasm for what they love will win the world? Why do we think that less passionate praise, less potent preaching, and less emphasis on His palpable presence are going to reach them? Here is what is true. When this world begins to walk into the houses of God and witnesses a people who truly love Him with all their heart and soul and mind and strength, who are passionate about Him, who want to be with Him more than they want to do what the rest of the world does with their time, and whose care and concern for their own dignity dissipates in the place of praise, that is when we will see a mass wave of salvation.

The Roman Empire witnessed the countercultural choices of Christians to remain in Rome during the plague, at risk and cost to their own lives, and the empire's head was turned. Similarly, when the Church stops exclaiming with their dead, dry, dutiful withholding in worship that God is not that great, but rather begins to break alabaster jars in lavish love for Him, proclaiming His greatness and gravity by their worship, it is then we'll see a moral and cultural revolution follow the revolution within.

? Shouldn't We Do Here What We Can't Do in Eternity?

One counter to the call of a first-love revolution will be, "I get where you're coming from, but shouldn't we do here, what we can't do there?" Meaning, shouldn't we do here, on earth, what we can't do there, in eternity? When that is said, what is meant? Saving the lost. Now, should we be about reaching the lost? Yes, because God is, and we are filled with His love to reach those He loves. But, is it true that this is the only thing we can do here but not in eternity? It is not. What else can we do here but not in eternity?

Hebrews 11:1 says, "Now faith is the assurance of *things* hoped for, the conviction of things not seen." In other words, faith is what we do before we see. Once we see God, we will no longer be responding in faith; simply stated, faith is not something we get to do in eternity. When the sky parts and Jesus is revealed at His return, yes, every knee will bow, but the opportunity for faith will have passed. Many of those knees will bow in acknowledgment, but acknowledgment is not faith. It does not please God, and it will not save.

When we enter into eternity, we will praise, but we won't be praising in faith, because faith is the gift we can only lay at God's feet before we see, not when we see, and certainly not after we see. How much does faith please God? He doesn't leave us guessing. He tells us in His Word, "[W]ithout faith it is impossible to please *Him*" (Hebrews 11:6). Also, consider this. What made Jesus marvel? In Matthew 8:10 we are told, "Now when Jesus heard *this*, He marveled and said to those who were following, 'Truly I say to you, I have not found such great faith with anyone in Israel.'" And when Jesus spoke about His return what was His concern? "'[W]hen the Son of Man comes, will He find faith on the earth?'" (Luke 18:8). Why is faith held in such high esteem by our Lord? Because what is uniquely possible here is uniquely pleasing there.

Think about the sacrifice of praise we're called to continually bring before Him here on earth. You cannot bring that same kind of sacrifice in eternity. Of Anna, we read in Luke 2, "She never left the temple, serving night and day with fastings and prayers" (Luke 2:37). We might say of an Anna who never leaves the house of God today that she is wasting her life away and neglecting the lost. Did God say that? Did He condemn her sacrifice? Instead, we see Him commend her as one who loved Him so much. We see God honor her life as one of the very first to have the Messiah revealed to her. Why? Think about it. A life like Anna's says to God, "Eternity is not enough time to praise You, not enough time to thank You, and not enough time to love You!"

With David, there was nowhere he wanted to be more than in the courts of the Lord. His love for the Lord and attentiveness to ministering to the Lord were exploited by Absalom. The people of Israel preferred the picture of a king at the gates, easily accessible, fraternizing with them, rather than one who was seeking the Lord's face. But, what did God say? He called David "'a man after His own heart'" (1 Samuel 13:14) and gave the Messianic line to him. That makes no sense if ministering to the heart of God in praise is a waste on earth since it's prevalent in Heaven!

What the Church has lost recognition of is that our love for God here, by faith, is not something that we can do there. Our worship of God while here, when we're not in Heaven, is a worship we'll never be able to bring Him again in Heaven. The sacrifice of praise we bring here is not one we can bring there. The incense of prayer offered in hope and faith here is not something we can bring there.

It is this, loving the One you have yet to see amidst a world that hates Him, that pleases God. As believers, it is our goal to bring to God what we will bring to Him once we see before we see! When we imagine ourselves worshiping God in Heaven, once we see face-to-face, if it does not match how we worship Him here, we have a missed opportunity to bring Him that praise by faith. When we imagine ourselves worshiping God in Heaven, when we do not have crying or suffering or mourning or pain, if it does not match how we worship Him now, we're missing this unique opportunity to bring Him a sacrifice of praise.

Will that hurt the cause of reaching the world? How ignorant! If we want Heaven to happen here perhaps we should start doing what Heaven does here! If God said He dwells in two places—the praises of His people and the gathering into Jesus name—perhaps we should clue in that to have the Kingdom of God here, we need the King who is God here.

? Hasn't the Gospel Always Been Contextualized?

You will likely hear people say, "But what about Paul saying, 'I have become all things to all men, so that I may by all means save some' (1 Corinthians 9:22)? Your insistence on using the words sin, repentance, obedience, and submission are keeping people from contextualizing the gospel."

By that same rationale, you can imagine that Paul would have pulled back from acknowledging Jesus as King over everything in a world where a claim to allegiance to another king was so unwelcome. But he didn't. When Paul became like a Jew or Gentile, he was saying he took on their culture and customs but not to the extent that he compromised the truth itself. Contextualization, Biblically, never compromises the truth. Biblical contextualization takes a truth and applies that truth accurately, illustrates that truth accurately, and explains that truth acccurately in a way that people can understand and comprehend without compromising it.

To contextualize the gospel, you have to retain the gospel. Otherwise, you are not contextualizing it but changing it. You cannot contextualize something and change the meaning of it at the same time. The gospel, without sin as moral wrong requiring the blood of Jesus Christ to atone for it, is not the gospel at all. If we change the meaning of sin to be something other than what sin is, we've not contextualized the gospel but compromised the gospel.

Now, when it comes to the word, "sin," there are other words that you can use for sin without distorting its Biblical meaning. For example, in some contexts, treason, rebellion, or hatred of God would carry the meaning quite well. To call sin moral wrong carries the original meaning of sin as well. However, none of these descriptors of sin would accomplish what the person who is looking to ease the gravity of sin over and smooth it out wants to do—make it less offensive. But, what we have to realize is, at the cost of making it less offensive to one party, we're making it more offensive to another, God. In doing so, we're putting up blockades on the path that would bring others into a relationship with Him.

Imagine a courtroom. A crime was committed against your family—a willful, violent crime. When the perpetrator takes the stand and addresses you, he says, "I made a mistake. I could have done better. I am a better person than that. We're all broken, and this was just my brokenness coming out. Can I have your forgiveness?" How would you feel about that? Do you see the problem? It's not repentance. It calls something that is morally reprehensible a mere misunderstanding.

We have many who think they've asked for God's forgiveness; but, they haven't, because they have never acknowledged sin as what it is—a moral wrong against their eternal and perfect Creator, which requires the blood of Jesus to atone and forgive.

There is much done in the name of contextualizing in order to reach the lost that is not Biblical. Throughout church history, the Church has come under the primary leadership of different gifts at different times. However, it has not been under the leadership of gifted apostles and prophets since the first century or two. There are times when it has come under the direction of administrators. There are times it has come under the teachers.

There are times it was led by the shepherds. In recent history, it has begun to be primarily influenced by leaders and evangelists (the two primary gifts needed to build a seeker-sensitive megachurch).

With every gift, when second love has been placed above first love, the direction of the grace gets redirected and perverted. When people are placed above praise, apostles either are sent away or they, themselves, direct their dogged determination not up, but in. They make themselves a force to be reckoned with. Prophets start to say, "Peace, peace," and bring encouragement but never correction. Shepherds put down the rod and staff and just pet the sheep. Teachers stick to insightful information but do not call for complete obedience. Those with the spiritual gift of healing do not consider it undeserved mercy but an entitlement by the gospel. Leaders become CEOs of a customer service agency. Mercy givers have compassion for people more so than the Lord and leave people in sin as a result.

What do evangelists do when not oriented rightly to true north? They reduce barriers to make the gospel more palatable to people. In other words, they become Heaven's salesmen and God's PR reps. They no longer rebuke sinners in their sermons, but they turn their rebukes away from the lost and toward the Church, even toward the Bible itself, or toward anything and anyone who is getting in the way of the lost liking us. To be clear, that is not a Biblical depiction of an evangelist, but every gifting gets perverted when it's not directed to keeping the first love first.

The true apostolic call on the Church in this hour is to throw away the broken compass, stop compromising the gospel in the name of contextualizing it, and return to true north, orienting every grace back up in first love. And when the world sees a Church who loves Him with all their hearts, praises Him with all their passion, and obeys Him with all their trust, then they will sit up and take notice that perhaps there is a God who is that great.

? Does Authenticity in Action Matter More than Action?

Authenticity has become an idol of this generation, manifesting the same way all idolatry does, as justification for withholding obedience from God. A first-love revolution is a head-on confrontation with the greatest idol of the Church—placing people on God's throne in His own house. All idols are sustained by status quo, and therefore, you should expect a full-out war in the heavenlies when you go to remove this idol.

When doing what God says is withheld, there is always an idol at work, and in this case, it is the idol of authenticity, an idol that essentially says in some form, "I am not going to do something I don't feel authentically." Saying this sounds noble and God-honoring—after all, we know God cares about the heart, not just external conformity—but is it? No, nothing that justifies disobedience is. It is simply a very deceptive idolized self, masquerading behind a virtue. It's why Paul never said, "I am a this. I am a that." Paul knew, "If I prize it, I am going to seek to prove it," and, "If I seek to prove it, I will give my loyalty to it." That is why he said in Galatians 2:20,

> I have been crucified with Christ; and it is no longer
> I who live, but Christ lives in me; and the *life* which I

now live in the flesh I live by faith in the Son of God, who loved me and gave Himself up for me.

To get really practical, let's say that my idolized self is that "I am rational." If I prize myself in being logical and reasonable, maybe even intelligent, what am I going to do when God does the miraculous, or when God does what doesn't make sense? Let's say, for example, God decides to speak in a way that is intellectually dissatisfying. What am I going to do? I am going to reject the miraculous speaking of God, because, "I am rational, and that's not rational." I am going to be committed to proving what I prize even at the expense of His praise.

Let's try a few others. Some people's idolized self is, "I am wise." They may ascribe their wisdom as coming from God, but they are only operating with worldly wisdom, which is basically always some form of hedonism—maximizing pleasure, prosperity, and popularity while minimizing pain, cost, and loss. When God calls them to do something that requires them to lay down their life, they take a pass. Why? Because, "That's not wise." They presume they are blessing God with their wisdom while they are rejecting Him, His will, and His ways.

Another person's idolized self may be sincerity: "I am sincere." But let's not overlook the fact that you can be sincerely wrong. The same is true with being moderate. "That thing that you say God is calling us to is extreme, but I am a moderate. That is who I am." But, consider this, you can be moderately indifferent to the things of God that you should be in awe of.

This same thing can happen with any idolized self, including being authentic, and this is one that, in our experience, the enemy loves to leverage a lot. We all know that Jesus condemned actions for show. We all know that God wants the heart, not just appearance and not just the action. If your idolized self is authentic, the enemy will leverage that all day to keep you away from the things that God has for you. The enemy will be quick to accuse you of doing what you are doing for show or of not having the right heart, all for one goal—to keep you from obeying, to keep you from responding, and to keep you from doing what God wants you to.

If we take the bait, where does it lead? We can respond to the miraculous in doubt or disbelief and say that we are being authentic as we do, or we can turn away from the things of the Spirit (and toward the flesh) and again, say that we're being authentic as we do. We forget that if human beings are being authentic to our humanity, we would never do what is holy, as we are authentically sinful, authentically disobedient, authentically disbelieving, authentically doubting, and authentically deserving of hell.

Do not be ruled by an idolized self of authenticity, and don't forget that Jesus said that obedience loves Him (John 14:15) and that obedience leads to our joy being complete (John 15:10–11). Christianity is both inside out and outside in. We obey when we feel like it. We also bring Him what He deserves even when we don't.

? Isn't an Emphasis on Obedience Legalism?

Another thing you might hear is, "What about Jesus whose burden is easy and whose yoke is light? You are turning walking with Jesus (with all of this emphasis on obedience) into more of an apostolic or Pauline hard, harsh, legalistic, and burdensome thing."

Obviously, this response comes from those who do not believe the Word of God is, well, the Word of God (as if the epistles are not the Word of God). That aside, is expecting full surrender and full obedience to God's commands legalistic, burdensome, and heavy? Is emphasis on obedience anti-grace, anti-gospel, and anti-Jesus? Some would say, "Yes," because of Jesus' statement in Matthew 11:30: "'For My yoke is easy and My burden is light.'" But is that right?

"Easy" is a very interesting translation choice by virtually every English translation out there. According to HELPS Word-studies[3], the meaning of the Greek word translated "easy" here is:

> **5543** *xrēstós* (an adjective, derived from 5530 /*xráo-mai*, "to furnish what is suitable, useful") – properly, *useful* (serviceable, productive); *well-fitted* (well-resourced); *useful* (beneficial, benevolent).
>
> On the spiritual plane, 5543 /xrēstós ("suitable, usefully kind") describes what God defines is *kind* and therefore also *eternally* useful! "We have no adjective in English that conveys this blend of being kind and good at the same time" (M. Vincent).

Isn't that interesting? The definition has nothing to do with the concept of ease at all! This word is translated as good or kind in every other verse where it is found, but, here it gets translated as "easy" over and over again. This is a case where the context is overly driving the translation of the word.

When people misportray this verse as justification for disobedience, they overlook the fact that Jesus actually speaks of a yoke. A yoke is a device used on a beast of burden so that it can pull a plow or some other heavy burden. Jesus didn't say, "My scarf is easy." He said yoke! And, as we have seen, Jesus did not say it was "easy." He said useful. Jesus contrasts His yoke with the yoke of the experts of the Law (that He had spoken about), a yoke that lays heavy burdens on men's shoulders (Matthew 23:4). How? By adding to the Law. Jesus was not rebuking those experts for teaching others to obey the Law that God gave. He was rebuking them for all the additions they made! That yoke leads to depletion and exhaustion.

Jesus, however, gives a yoke that yokes you to who? Him! To requote HELPS Word-studies that is what God defines as "*kind* and therefore also *eternally* useful."[4] What Jesus called "heavy" was adding to what God requires. But, what people call "heavy" today is very different—now, simple obedience to God is called "heavy." So many think that Jesus' "light" yoke means that you don't have to obey God. Let's be honest. That is just stupid, but idolatry makes us really dumb with the Word of God.

It's worth also noting that the "light" yoke referenced here is from the Greek word "ἐλαφρός" (pronounced el-af-ros'), which is only used in one other place in the New Testament. It's in 2 Corinthians 4:17, which references their "momentary, *light* affliction" (emphasis added). Whatever "affliction" is perceived by the Church from loving God with all is far less than the affliction referenced as "light" then!

All to say, Scripture expects the servants of our Lord to actually obey the Lord. Those who know the Scriptures know that obedience is God's love language, that obedience is not legalism, and that it is not a heavy burden. It is precisely the yoke, which is good for them, eternally useful, fits, and lifts!

? Full Surrender at the Start?

This call to full surrender in love for the One who loved us first will be met with criticism by some. They will object to the idea of full surrender on account of the process of sanctification. They will rightly point out that there is no such thing as microwave Christianity and that all of us are in the process of being transformed into the likeness of Christ. That is true, but the process of sanctification and the starting line of full surrender are not incompatible with one another.

The truth is that the process of growing in Christ and becoming like Christ is a continual process of full surrender. As God reveals more, we respond to the more with full surrender. It's good for us to recognize that this process will never stop. No matter how much we have of God, no matter how much we know of God, there is infinitely more of Him to have and to know. As God reveals more of Himself, He is going to illuminate areas where we are not yet conformed to the image of Christ and that will call for surrender again.

Here's what must be clear. A process of continual full surrender is different than choosing which pieces we're going to give God and which pieces we're going to withhold from Him. Full surrender does not say, "Okay, I'll obey Him in this, but not in that." Full surrender says, "All of it is His," even if it doesn't know, comprehend, or understand all that is entailed in all.

Those who oppose the call for full surrender in Christian discipleship will say, "Look at the disciples! They were screw-ups, weren't they? At what point would you have counted them as disciples?" It would be at the point Jesus said, "Drop your nets," and they did, at once, immediately, and entirely. They did not say, "Not my nets." If they had said that, Jesus would not have said, "Well, that's okay. You can still be my disciples without doing what I just told you." He is either Lord, or He isn't. That is not to say that Jesus wasn't going to call them to additional steps, and that is not to say there wasn't ongoing growth. But, they obeyed fully what they knew fully.

Contrast that to the rich young man. There could be reason to believe he was actually more well-versed in Scripture and more impressive on a religious level than the disciples themselves. However, he was not willing to do what he knew. He walked away greatly distressed (Matthew 19:22), and then Jesus taught on the impossibility of the rich entering the Kingdom of Heaven.

Full surrender is the starting line. It is the finish line. It is the standard every step of the way. When we are saved, we surrender all we know, and every day thereafter, we grow in our knowledge of God's will generally for all believers and specifically for our lives. Every day requires new surrender. Yes, we're a work in process, but full surrender is the standard all along the way. As soon as we say, "No," to God, we are halted in our sanctification until we repent and turn that, "No," into a, "Yes." It's about being obedient to all that you know. We cannot raise up disciples who love Him with all while making concessions in the area of obedience to all. Jesus was clear. If we love Him, we will obey His commands (John 14:15).

? What about Loving God with Our Minds?

Another set of questions you may hear is, "With all the emphasis on inquiring prayer, aren't you contradicting the command to love God with all our minds? After all, if God gave us reason, understanding, and the gift of thinking, wouldn't He want us to use those?"

Granted, most of the time, this kind of thing isn't said so outright. It's concealed in more carefully crafted statements. For example, several years ago, a man was serving on the board of a Christian ministry. He made a decision. Someone asked him if he had prayed about it, and he said, "I don't need to. I prayed at the beginning of the day for God to direct my thinking, and I trust that He does." Is that true? Is every thought we have from God? Surely, it is not.

But, for many leaders, who often become leaders because of their strategic minds and decision-making quality, for them to submit their own logic and decision-making prowess to wait on God to speak to someone or through someone else (and then many times in a way that is counterintuitive) is humbling and is experienced as a major loss of their voice.

By the way, this right here is why Moses was considered the most humble man on earth (Numbers 12:3). He never claimed to do anything based on his own smarts, skills, strategy, or wisdom. The natural man or woman wants to be seen as significant, as valuable, and as making a unique contribution, but Moses did not. He was the most humble man, precisely because he went up on the mountain to get answers! When God is up on a mountain, and you go up and your function is to hear what He has to say and repeat it, that is humbling. There was no guesswork. Nobody was thinking, "Wow! Moses is so smart! Where does this wisdom come from?" Moses was simply carrying out the orders of another. (Ironically, this idea is now portrayed as the thing a prideful leader does.)

This is also what we saw modeled in Christ. Jesus never tried to differentiate Himself from the Father in order to show His unique contribution. Jesus said in John that He only says what the Father says (John 12:49) and only does what the Father is doing (John 5:19). How many Christian leaders would be willing to be that submitted of a middleman and have others know about it? No sermon would ever demonstrate their own skills or unique creative contributions anymore! Could they handle that?

Along these lines, the New Testament word for preaching is to "herald." In ancient times, kings would have heralds. Yet, we don't know who these heralds were. Why? They did not display their own creativity, wisdom, or oratorical ability. Instead, they heralded what the king told them to say. That is the highest form of preaching—when we take no pride in what we preached, because we heard from the Lord what He wanted said and simply heralded that message. Now, does that mean we should not study or prepare ahead of time? No, we can herald a message much closer to the Lord's heart when hours are spent praying and listening rather than standing up and just expecting God to fill our mouths as we open them.

But, back to the point about being led by God, even when we are leading others. True leaders in Christ understand that they are those under authority. What if each of us saw our chief responsibility of leading as getting with God (not in isolation only, but with others as well), hearing what He wants, and setting out to see that happen? Moses did that. That is humble leadership, which submits its understanding to the Lord's leading.

Can you imagine how different things would be if we didn't just pray the prayer, "Your kingdom come, Your will be done on earth as it is in heaven," but we actually asked Him what His will was and then made that our aim for each gathering, for each day, and for each meeting?

How many service debriefs do you think that God sits through and hears conclusions that He hasn't come to? Who is evaluating a gathering by asking, "What was in God's heart to do, and did that happen?" In many rooms, if you asked that question, people could not even answer it outside of general principles (the Word was preached, worship was sung, etc.). Technical excellence doesn't make a service a success. It can reduce barriers by not being distracting, but that is not what makes a gathering a success. God getting what God wants makes a service, a gathering, a success. But, all too often, our decision-making and evaluating look just like the world's, and that is a problem.

Here's another example of how this objection about losing the stewarding of our minds might come across. We've also heard people say in response to prophetic words that had been tested and released, "You need to hold these prophetic words loosely. Don't you believe

God has given us a mind of wisdom and that His wisdom is flowing through what we're saying?" (Of course, they said this as their wisdom contradicted the call of God spoken through the prophetic words.)

The concept of asking God, waiting on God, hearing from Him, and making decisions based upon what God says will be wildly unliked by those who dislike decisions that flow from that place. After all, isn't "going up on a mountain and coming down with a decision" a derogatory concept in Christendom today? The flesh of man wants to walk by sight and not by the faith that comes by hearing.

If our wisdom is no different than the world's wisdom and is based on maximizing our satisfaction, security, and significance while minimizing cost, we should not be so quick to assume it's the wisdom of God at all. After all, how many so-called unwise things did God call people to do in Scripture? Doesn't God say, "'For My thoughts are not your thoughts, / Nor are your ways My ways,' declares the Lord" (Isaiah 55:8)? The Bible is filled with those who ran ahead based on their own thinking but did not inquire of the Lord or seek His direction. As a result, Heaven's stamp of approval did not come down on them or their actions. The Bible is also filled with those who heard the prophetic word and did not heed it, and Heaven's stamp of approval did not come down on them either.

Inquiring of God—and being led by Him, even when His direction is counterintuitive—is not devaluing the mind. It is putting our understanding in its proper place, below God's. The one with true understanding and wisdom is the one who wants to hear from God and do what He says. Loving God with our minds is about bringing them into submission and alignment with Him, His will, and His ways. When our every thought is taken captive and submitted to Him, we are loving Him with our minds. When our thoughts are filled with thanksgiving, praise, and affection, we are loving Him with our minds. When we assume our thoughts are His, we are not loving Him with our minds.

This change from operating out of natural logic and strategic thinking to following the Spirit is not an easy one for the flesh. Our team could honestly tell you that the more we all inquired of God, the more all of us felt like we lost at least a piece of our voice or our unique contribution that we brought to the table. As leaders, we love to solve problems. As leaders, we love to set the direction. But, to become more like Christ, who sought to only say what God said, how God said it, and only do as God was doing, it's a bigger loss (naturally speaking) for a leader than most would realize.

Yet, as we lose our own voice, we magnify His. We go from, "What do I think?" to, "What does He think?" We go from, "What do I want to do?" to, "What does He want done?" We go from, "What do I want to say, how do I want to say it, and when do I want to say it?" to, "What does He want to say, how does He want to say it, and when does He want to say it?"

When our own thinking is submitted to Him, it honors Him. It is here we come into alignment with the stream of His Spirit. When what we say is what God wants to say and when He wants to say it, there is more power. When what we do is what God wants to do and when He wants to do it, there is greater presence. For so many, the cloud of glory and pillar of fire have moved on, but they remain camped in a former place of habitation.

Without returning to being sons and daughters of God led by the Spirit of God, we're often building churches on dried-up ocean beds, walking on fossils, and lacking the rain. Because of that, we cannot get it to "work" except by building a Ferris wheel of entertainment in the place that was once occupied by His presence.

? What about a Balanced Life?

The call to all rubs against another commonly embraced notion in cultural Christianity, the belief that we're to have a balanced life—with God first, family second, health third, work fourth, or whatever variation of these priorities. It is true that, in Ecclesiastes, we are told, "There is an appointed time for everything" (Ecclesiastes 3:1), but recognizing there is a time for everything isn't the same as parceling our lives out in such a way that we have our well-balanced pie of God and our other priorities. God is not first among many. He is all. He is everything. Everything else—including our marriages, our families, our work, and our activities—exists to serve Him.

This might sound like a small distinction, but it's not. When there is a first, second, and third, there ends up being a competition for resources rather than an alignment of them. The greatest commandment to love God with all will never be lived by someone who is saying, "That's fine, as long as my second and third priority get the portion of the pie that I think they should."

We are to be those who do all of our work as if working for God Himself (Colossians 3:23–24), for the glory of God. We are to be those who lead and teach our families to love God with all of their hearts, all of their strength, all of their minds, and all of their souls. Our marriages and families are intended to be a primary place where we live the mission with every decision. We are to love God with all our strength as well. Yet, we live in a world that cannot do that, because such exertion isn't good for their body. So, they love their body, but not God with all their body. (Reread Paul's list of sufferings in 2 Corinthians 11:22–28 and consider how many would correct him for living an imbalanced life, yet, God commends his sacrifice!)

In place of all, we've settled for saying, "Put God first." Yet, what is left for God in the pie isn't enough to even live the basic Biblical Christian life! We subdivide and subcategorize and because of that, we inherently fall short of the First and Greatest Commandment. It's worth acknowledging that over the years, we have had the privilege of serving alongside many from the persecuted church, and we can tell you that we've never heard them talk about balance. (By the way, when what we are preaching or professing doesn't apply to all Christians in all contexts, we need to check what we are preaching.)

The standard is to love God with all in every single domain of our lives. That said, we admit that most marriages are somewhat unequally yoked and due to that, if one person wants to be all in for the Lord at all times, but the other does not, it does result in divided interests. That is not God's original design, of course. God would not have instituted marriage with Adam and Eve as an institution that inherently would divide their heart's aim to please Him. But, 1 Corinthians 7 acknowledges that in a fallen world, this is a reality (1 Corinthians 7:32-35). Even then, at all times, our individual goal must be to love God with all to the extent it depends on us. And, even when compromises are inevitable (i.e., my husband won't allow us to tithe on our full income), we still love God with all so far as it depends on us (i.e., the wife tithing on her portion of the income).

Part of the hidden resistance to a life of all is the underlying belief that life here is better than there and that something lost here won't gain more there. When we have a faulty view of eternity, it puts undue pressure to have here what cannot be had there. In truth, anything given up for His name's sake here is gained there, and nothing kept here is gained there (Matthew 6:19–21; Matthew 10:42; Mark 10:29).

A first-love revolution is not to put God first. Everyone believes they are doing that. A first-love revolution is to put the First and Greatest Commandment first, a commandment to love God with all, not a portion.

? We Can Only Repent of So Much, Right?

Some will say that a continuous call to repentance cannot be sustained, that there is only so much repenting that you can do, and then you are done. I (Shane) will never forget an incident from years ago. I was speaking to a man, and he said, "I've done all the repenting I can. I literally can't think of another thing to repent of. I don't want to hear about repentance anymore." Of course, I was thinking to myself, "Do you need some help? I can think of several things, including what you just said!" Haha! Don't worry, I did not say that. But, I can tell you I was shocked that a respected member of a church would say such a thing. That kind of statement is problematic on so many levels, the least of which is not 1 John 1:8: "If we say that we have no sin, we are deceiving ourselves and the truth is not in us."

But, for the sake of argument, let's say that was a genuine statement and that you really were not aware of anything else to repent of in your life. Should you find that comforting and as a cause to coast? Should you assume that your lack of knowledge of sin equates to an actual lack of existence of sin? Or should you turn to God in desperation, praying what David did?

> Search me, O God, and know my heart;
> Try me and know my anxious thoughts;
> And see if there be any hurtful way in me,
> And lead me in the everlasting way (Psalm 139:23–24).

When we think we lack sin, we certainly lack something, but it's not sin, it is a searching of the heart.

A lack of known areas in need of repentance reveals that we have not had our hearts searched by God, but it also reveals we lack increased knowledge of God. Any increased revelation of God will undoubtedly result in an increased awareness and understanding of the depths of our sin. Did Isaiah know his sin before the revelation of the throne room the same way he did after (Isaiah 6:5)? Of course not.

A first-love revolution must not underemphasize obedience, as obedience is God's love language. An emphasis on obedience inevitably emphasizes repentance. If the loving and kind call to repentance is not appreciated by all, do not divert or distort the message. No one ever comes to the end of repentance in this life, because no one ever gets to the end of their knowledge of Him.

? Isn't Scripture Sufficient?

When some hear an emphasis on the power of God, the presence of God, or even the prophetic, they might challenge your belief in the sufficiency of Scripture: "Don't you believe that Scripture is fully sufficient?" Is that what a first-love revolution is saying?

For starters, the term "sufficiency of Scripture" and the actual theological meaning of this term sometimes get confused. In coining this phrase, theologians never imagined that we could not benefit from anything outside of Scripture (such as math or medicine). The point of this doctrine is that the Bible is the sole authoritative revelation to which everything pertaining to Christian faith and practice must submit. To understand where this doctrine came from, you need to remember that the Reformation was countering the Catholic claims regarding tradition and papal authority.

Scripture is authoritative. It is what God has chosen to reveal of Himself in all times and all places, and in that regard, it is sufficient to reveal Him, who He is, and what is required for salvation. But, God never said that He would not speak beyond and act beyond what is contained in the Scriptures. God will never contradict who He is as revealed in His Word. In that way, the Scriptures are authoritative. The Bible is the Word of God. It reveals God. However, it is not the equivalent of God. The Bible is not God's box that He cannot speak or act outside of, meaning, it is not true that everything He will ever say has already been said or everything He will ever do has already been done. He is alive, at work, and active. He is still the same God today as He was and is on every page of Scripture.

To claim that Scripture's sufficiency has forever muzzled God from speaking and restricted God from leading His sons and daughters is actually a betrayal of the sufficiency of Scripture to accurately reveal who God is. He has never been that God. He never will be. To claim He is, is a betrayal of the one authoritative revelation of the person of God, which is the Scripture.

Furthermore, to say that all we need is Scripture and not the Spirit of God, not the power and presence of God at work in our lives, is wrong. Yes, the role of the Word of God is critical and crucial. We are told,

> All Scripture is inspired by God and profitable for teaching, for reproof, for correction, for training in righteousness; so that the man of God may be adequate, equipped for every good work (2 Timothy 3:16-17).

Scripture is sufficient and essential for these purposes. However, don't miss what God says in 2 Peter:

> Grace and peace be multiplied to you in the knowledge of God and of Jesus our Lord; seeing that *His divine power has granted to us everything pertaining to life and godliness*, through the true knowledge of Him who called us by His own glory and excellence (2 Peter 1:2–3, emphasis added).

What has granted to us everything pertaining to life and godliness? What has given us what we need to live the life that God calls us to live? God's divine power.

In summary, in His authoritative Word, God did not say, "It's all Word only," or, "It's all Spirit only." It's Word and Spirit. Is the Word of God sufficient in that it is authoritative? Yes. But should the Word of God, as sufficient in that manner, be seen as a substitution for the Spirit or a limitation on God, meaning He can never speak or act beyond what He already has? Of course not. To believe that the power, presence, and speaking of God are as essential today as God reveals them to be in Scripture is not to challenge the sufficiency of Scripture but to uphold the authority of Scripture that teaches such.

? Is It a Sin Not to Sing?

Because we believe that God not only tells us to praise Him but also how to praise Him, this comes as a shock to many and they ask, "Wait! Are you saying that if I do not dance every time I come to worship, I am sinning?"

When it comes to the Biblical standards of worship, so much of our instruction regarding worship is, of course, found in the Psalms and other places in the Old Testament. We acknowledge that virtually nobody else perceives that Old Testament standards for worship apply today. For most, if it's not repeated in the New Testament, it does not apply. We, however, believe this position is theologically untenable by the letter, and certainly by the spirit, of the law. We believe that the New Testament standard for worship should be higher, not lower, than the Old.

That said, many find most of what is included in the Psalms and elsewhere regarding how we are called to worship somewhat palatable. However, certainly, there are commands that many find difficult to embrace, and perhaps none more so than the call to dance in worship.

So, how do we approach such a command? When it comes to this particular command, there are only two scriptures that call us to bring dancing into worship (Psalm 149:3; Psalm 150:4). Beyond that, there are examples of those who chose to do so, but they are stated descriptively, not prescriptively. We are never to go beyond what is written in creating requirements. God does not say that we must dance every time we get together to worship. That said, it is not a sin if someone does not dance in one of God's worship gatherings. That is the letter of the Law.

The spirit of the Law, however, is to love God with all our heart, soul, mind, and strength. The spirit of the Law is to worship by faith before we see Him face to face as if we were before Him face to face! We only get one chance to do that. So, when 95% of churches have never had even one person dance before the Lord in His worship, that is a problem. When 99% of believers have never danced before the Lord in praise, not even once in their lives, that is a problem.

At the heart level, we dream of a day when the world steps into a church and the praise testifies to the gravity and greatness of God. As it stands today, His people have much more praise for the things of this world than for Him, and much worship testifies that God is not that great and not that good. The heart's burden is for God to get His glory. But, the letter of the law (in our view) is simply that God's praise should include all His Word calls for (singing, clapping, kneeling, dancing, shouting, etc.) but does not prescribe how often.

For us personally, as leaders in the church, we want to lead God's people the way King David did. We want the church's praise to catch the attention of Heaven and be found pleasing to Him. We prefer to err on the side of maximums versus minimums. So yes, for us, we do try to get our face to the ground, knees to the ground, to shout and to clap and to sing and to dance virtually every time we worship. We do not prescribe that. It's not required. It's a freewill offering. In truth, we also ask the Holy Spirit to give us an idea of an offering that we can bring in worship that is not commanded anywhere in Scripture, something truly beyond the requirements. Why? We're trying to capture the heart of worship.

All to say, we would say that a believer who never does what is commanded in worship does sin. We would not, however, prescribe a frequency or setting for that where God's Word does not. But, of course, the heart is not just to avoid sin but to bless God. That is what we're after.

? Isn't Apostleship Only a Part of the Past?

Some in the Church assume that apostleship is dead and only applied to a small set of people in the first century. We, however, do believe that the spiritual gifts of apostleship and prophecy are very much available and critical to the health of the Church today.

In contrast to the New Apostolic Reformation (NAR), which believes the offices of apostle and prophet are being restored today, we do not mean the office of prophet as we read in the Old Testament or the office of apostle given directly by Jesus in the New Testament. When we speak about apostleship and prophecy, we are referring to the spiritual gifts of apostleship and prophecy, not to offices. Both of these gifts were attributed to a number of individuals in the New Testament, and when it comes to apostleship, that is true of those who were not one of the capital "A" apostles (Acts 14:14; Romans 16:7; 2 Corinthians 8:23 [often translated "messengers" or "representatives" is literally "apostles"]; Philippians 2:25 [often translated "messenger" is literally "apostle"]; 1 Corinthians 4:6–10).

The Church is meant to be led by those through whom the spiritual graces of apostleship and prophecy flow (1 Corinthians 12:28). Because the spiritual gift of prophecy is less contested, we are going to spend our time addressing the spiritual gift of apostleship here.

So, what was/is the spiritual gift of apostleship? The word for apostle means "a sent one." To understand the uniqueness of this gift, we need to understand this term. To be sent emphasizes the authority of the One who is doing the sending. (There were many other word options to carry the meaning of being sent, being a messenger, being a servant, and being a herald. However, this word uniquely tied one back to the authority of the sender.) If you are sent by, you are in service to. Imagine two people standing in front of you today. One says, "I am a teacher of the Bible." The other says, "I am a sent one." Where does the gravity of your understanding lie about the second? It's clear. They are under authority. They are defined in relationship to the one who sent them. It's not an authority of their own initiative. Apostles are under His authority, commissioned by Him, and sent by Him.

We have lost the force of this gift by transliterating the Greek word apostolos, instead of translating the word.

In our world of rugged and radical individualism, the connection between being sent and being under authority is somewhat foreign. It stems from a context we no longer have today. Prior to and under the Roman Empire, kingdoms' territories were expanded as generals were sent by their king to take territory and establish the kingdom in a new location. The soldiers under the general were not thought of as sent ones, because their commanding officer was not at a distance. The sent one was the one who left, went out, and then reported directly back to the one who sent him. When the New Testament picks up the term, "sent one," the connotation of being under authority would not have been lost. The apostles are like generals who were *sent* by their King to take territory and turn it into a society under the authority of their King!

You can recognize those with the gift of apostleship, in large part, because they have similar traits to generals who would be sent to establish the kingdom in a new place. They tend to carry a unique fortitude to be on mission, under authority, and even in the most hostile environments that would pressure many to compromise, apostles remain uncompromising. Just as generals in the army may not be the best snipers, tank drivers, ship captains, or the best in any other particular skill, they tend to be generals for their uncompromising adherence to the orders of their commanding officer, higher capacity for stress and difficulty, leadership by example, and desire to be at war in lieu of remaining stationed.

Apostleship, contrary to how it is sometimes discussed in some circles today, is a humble thing, because "sent one" says nothing about the one sent, but much about the One who sent. It's a humble thing to be defined in relationship to another, but that is what the spiritual gift means. If you are sent by, you are in service to. If you are sent by, you do whatever the sending One wants done, wherever you go.

Those with the spiritual gift of apostleship can be recognized by a dogged determination to see God's will and God's ways enacted on location. They are utterly determined to see the rule of the One who sent them applied where they are sent. Yes, it can be a new area geographically, but it can also be new ground in the same area. Are they radical? Yes. Are they bulldozers? Yes. Are they obsessed with God's glory and at risk of ignoring people's needs? Yes. And so, they should have prophets, evangelists, shepherds, and teachers around them to supplement what they lack without a doubt. But, the apostles are first, because they orient the whole body up, toward the One in authority, for the glory of God, first.

If your local church leadership isn't led by those with the graces of apostleship and prophecy, the compass will struggle to stay true north. Evangelists often experience an incessant pull to reorient the Church out toward the lost. Shepherds and teachers often feel an incessant pull to reorient it down towards the sheep. Those with the graces of apostleship and prophecy are necessary to orient the compass true north, and other giftings do better at staying true north under their leadership. Picture a funnel being oriented directly up toward Heaven versus at an angle. The level of outpouring is in relationship to the angle of the funnel. (This, by the way, is why ministries that have someone with apostleship at the forefront often have signs, wonders, miracles, and manifestations of the presence and power of God.)

If you are the leader and this isn't your gifting, there are several ways to supplement what is lacking. One way is to position someone with this grace in close proximity to you, perhaps as an associate pastor or executive pastor. If you do this, it's important that you give that person explicit permission to constantly remind you and others who it's about (Him) and continually challenge you and others to go after what is not yet gained for His glory. We all need to rely on the grace of God flowing through others (as none of us has all the gifts). This is no different; it perhaps just requires more intentionality.

The other two options are a bit more extreme and should only be done with God's explicit leading. One of those is to change positions, becoming the teacher or pastor under a new lead pastor with this grace, or to come under another church where those with these spiritual graces are already in place. In summary, Ephesians says,

> And He gave some *as* apostles, and some *as* prophets, and some *as* evangelists, and some *as* pastors and teachers, for the equipping of the saints for the work of service, to the building up of the body of Christ (Ephesians 4:11–12).

In the Church, just as in the global Church, we want all five of these graces operating, according to God's design, in the greatest measure possible for Him to receive the most praise possible.

Part V

Closing Thoughts

14

A Final Word

Jesus taught two parables to portray the separation of the wise and foolish. One is found in Matthew 7, "The Parable of the Two Foundations." The other is in Matthew 25, "The Parable of Ten Virgins." The fool in the first parable is the one "'who hears these words of Mine and does not act on them'" (Matthew 7:26). The fools in the second parable are those who "'took no oil with them'" (Matthew 25:3). In the first parable, the fool is the one who lacked obedience to the teachings of the Lord. In the second, the fools are those who lacked dependence upon the Spirit.

The consequences of being foolish in these two parables could not be stated much more disastrously. For the one, "'The rain fell, and the floods came, and the winds blew and slammed against that house; and it fell—and great was its fall'" (Matthew 7:27). For the other, the following happened:

"And while they were going away to make the purchase, the bridegroom came, and those who were ready went in with him to the wedding feast; and the door was shut. Later the other virgins also came, saying, 'Lord, lord, open up for us.' But he answered, 'Truly I say to you, I do not know you.' Be on the alert then, for you do not know the day nor the hour" (Matthew 25:10–13).

Jesus could not have been clearer about the danger of being a fool.

In both cases, we have a picture of the foolish being those who did not persevere in faith, who were not ready, and who were not saved. While we recognize some would interpret that to mean they were never saved and others would interpret that to mean they lost their salvation, if we can put differences aside momentarily, we can mutually agree on the gravity of the situation. In both parables, the percentage of those lost was half. And, who were those that were lost? In the "Parable of the Two Foundations," they were those who heard the words of Christ! In the "Parable of Ten Virgins," they were those who waited and watched for the bridegroom, carried a burning lamp that had oil in it, and even said, "Lord, lord!"

Jesus taught us so well. We truly have no excuse, and yet, we have much of Christendom attempting to get away with the very things Jesus warned us would lead to disastrous eternal outcomes. So many are attempting to walk by the light of His Word, but they are not sufficiently depending on His Spirit by coming to have the lampstand refilled daily with fresh oil. Will they not, in the end, be those whose lamps go out, unable to sustain from a lack of seeking and purchasing of fresh oil? Jesus emphatically portrays for us a picture of many who are expecting to enter into the Kingdom of God, even desiring to enter the Kingdom of God, and yet failing to keep the lamp burning due to a lack of oil.

For those not relying on the power and presence of God, but ignorantly assuming that whatever is required is happening automatically, they need to wake up. Eternities are on the line. God has given us everything that we need to be the Church that He has called us to be and live the lives that He has called us to live. But if we do not make much of the grace that He has given, of what He alone provides and supplies, we will find ourselves in lack. Our churches will be dead and dry, in short supply of the presence of God. Our lives, at best, will be marked by apathy, indifference, weakness, and a lack of spiritual vitality. Instead of loving God with all our hearts, we will have caverns for hearts.

Simultaneously, much of the Church today loves to hear the Word of God, but they do not love to obey the Word of God. Oh, how many love a good Bible study but walk in sin! Jesus taught so clearly. The foolish one whose house will not stand on the day of testing is the one "'who hears these words of Mine and does not act on them'" (Matthew 7:26). For believers who neglect to read, reflect upon, and respond to Scripture on their own, wake up! For teachers who love to give people insights and illuminations, but do not call people to repentance and obedience, wake up!

To persevere in faith, we must walk in the light of God's Word, actually obeying Him, while relying on the Spirit to do so. Yet, there is great segregation in the Church today, between Word churches and Spirit churches. Often they despise and disdain one another. The truth is that both Word and Spirit churches tend to see themselves as superior to the other and can even be boastful about how they are not like the other. Rather than seeing the singularity of what they are as indicative of what they lack, they perceive it as a statement of superiority.

As those who have spent time around both streams, we would say that there are things on both sides that are truly superior to the other and things on both sides that are truly inferior to the other. It's time for the streams to come together. The Word is not for some. The Spirit is not for others. Some do not just need the Word, while others just need the Spirit. God's design is not Word or Spirit, but Word and Spirit.

It is time for us to recognize that there are both oaks and elms in the Kingdom of God, meaning what? Oak trees grow consistently over time. They can thrive in almost any climate, even with little water. They are steady, strong, and not easily swayed by the wind. They are like the oaks of righteousness referenced in Isaiah 61:3. Elms are different. Elm trees tend to grow by streams and by rivers. They shoot up quickly, but they need a lot of water. They are strong too but bend in the breeze more easily than oaks. If you saw a video of an oak tree in a storm, you may see its leaves shaking a little and its branches barely moving, and you might falsely conclude the wind and rain were light. In contrast, if you saw an elm in that same storm, you might perceive that a hurricane had hit!

The Church, by and large, has become two different groves of trees—the oaks here and the elms there, and yes, the oak groves are the Word churches and the elm groves are the Spirit churches. It is time for oaks and elms to begin to flourish around the same riverbed of God's Spirit.

To do this we need to acknowledge that some people are wired more like oaks, very left-brained, whereas others more naturally fit in with elms, very right-brained. When the wind (i.e., the Spirit) is blowing and the rain is coming down as in times of revival, oaks and elms will be in the same space but will tend to have a very different experience. Both will thrive, but elms will be in Heaven while oaks will be concerned that they aren't keeping their normal daily rhythms! Out of season, however, when the rains and winds are lighter than desired, oaks may bear up better, because their roots are deep by the stream (Psalm 1:3).

When God moves mightily, it may look different for the two. Elms are going to talk about the hurricane of God's Spirit wrecking them. Oaks are going to say, "It was a good service. I definitely think I felt something. Yeah, it was good." While we would admit there tend to be personality differences that contribute to the types of churches people feel more comfortable or natural in and therefore choose, we contend that it is unacceptable for any church to be Word or Spirit, oak or elm. Oaks need water. Elms need roots. Is the Kingdom of God a matter of wiring, personality, or preference? It is not.

Our prayer is for a revolution that returns to its roots, yielding a Church that is wise as defined in God's eyes and overcomes for the praise of His name, a Church with a persevering faith. For that to happen, we must know His Word and obey His Word. For that to happen, we also must come daily to be freshly filled with the oil of His Spirit. One without the other will not do. We must build our churches to be full Word and full Spirit, for His glory.

Part VI

Appendices

Appendix A

A Call to Break What Is Broken (Governance)

You've heard about the revolution that we believe is absolutely urgent and essential for the Church. If you go down this path, you're going to need to change your structures, systems, and policies, because they, as they are today, support the status quo of today.

A critical component of this is to break what is broken in the Church—governance. Of course, only those in these positions have the authority to actually change it, so this chapter is written to all the board members of churches out there whose pastors have a burning in their heart toward a revolution that returns to first love.

Historically, there have been two different approaches to board governance when it comes to the Church. One is to have a board of remote participants, pastors, and leaders who provide accountability on a quarterly or annual basis. The other approach has been to have a board of volunteers from the church, often labeled the elder board. Many have moved away from the second in favor of the first due to the amount of horror stories out there. But, are these the only two options, and should we continue to think about elders in this way?

Is the elder system of many churches today Biblical? Let's take a look. Even a short study of the New Testament reveals the following:

- The elders oversaw the finances of the church (Acts 11:29–30).
- The terms, elder and pastor, were used interchangeably, and the elders did the work of pastoring. Elder was not a position separated from the actual responsibility of pastoring (1 Peter 5:1–2).
- The terms elder, pastor, and overseer were all used interchangeably (1 Peter 5:1-2; Titus 1:5,7).
- The elders were those who were in leadership and who led the way. (In 1 Timothy 5:17, the word, "rule well," is from the Greek word for "leading the way," and it is the same word for the gift of leadership in Romans 12:8).
- In Romans 12:8, leaders are exhorted to lead diligently. The word "diligently" comes from the Greek word, σπουδή (pronounced spoo-day'), which means, "'to make haste' and is thus closely related to 'to be zealous, active, concerned about something.'"[1] You cannot lead without setting the pace. We all know this. Inherently when you have someone who puts in less time, effort, and diligence leading someone who puts in more time, effort, and diligence, it causes problems. Elders who rule well would be better translated as those who "lead rightly." All elders should be gifted leaders as a baseline.
- All elders must be able to teach (1 Timothy 3:2; Titus 1:9). Some elders labor strenuously in the Word and

> teaching (1 Timothy 5:17). (The ability to teach Bib-
> lically is not necessarily the ability to communicate
> to a room full of people as we think of it.)

So, in summary, in the Bible, what do we see? The overseer/elder pastors were those senior-most pastoral leaders of the church, who carried the most responsibility in the church. They were called to be pastors, graced with spiritual gifts of leadership along with equipping/oversight gifts. They set the pace in their labor and of the work of the church, teaching or shepherding and laboring day in and day out. They served as decision-makers, directing and determining the course of the ministry (in line with God), and did not outsource that to others.

We don't read of others, who were people in their congregations (like Alexander the metalworker, Priscilla the purple dyer, Cornelius the security guy, or whatever other important fields they might be in) being elected to become the "elders" for a few years, and therefore, showing up to preside over those who were laboring day in and day out and set the direction for the church.

We need to be honest. The way the Church is labeling and installing "elders" or similar board types is often wildly unbiblical to the point that it's beyond ridiculous. Pastors, who are the true elders overseeing the major ministries of the church, must have the authority to follow the Lord within Biblical boundaries. It's a very dangerous divide to separate elder from pastor. When you put the appeal of power in front of people without the pain, perseverance, and consequence of responsibility, watch out.

There is a dangerous divide in much of the Church today. Spiritual leaders are installed into positions, but the volunteer board possesses the spiritual authority, direction, and decision-making of the church. Although church attenders don't hear about it often, there are many, many stories of terminations and splits happening as a result.

A pastor should be able to say, "I've heard God saying . . ." and, assuming that it aligns with Scripture and God's character as revealed in Scripture, he/she should then have the authority to lead the church in alignment with that. (They should also have other elders praying and testing with them before committing to anything significant.) That is not out of line with Scripture but in line with it. In contrast, a traditional elder board, made of volunteer leaders saying, "We don't care what you are hearing," or, "We are not going to do that," or, "We are the authority, so you can't," is not Biblical.

That brings us to the crux of the dangerous divide. What is a pastor supposed to do in that situation? Consider the example set in Scripture. In Acts 4, the rulers, elders, and scribes were gathered in Jerusalem, and they exhorted Peter and John to stop speaking or teaching in the name of Jesus Christ. What do Peter and John do in response?

> But Peter and John answered and said to them, "Whether it is right in the sight of God to give heed to you rather than to God, you be the judge; for we cannot stop speaking about what we have seen and heard" (Acts 4:19–20).

Some would look at this scenario and conclude Peter and John were insubordinate. But were they? God never calls us or commands us to be submissive to another at the cost of being faithful to Him. Furthermore, if being faithful to God requires a sacrifice of something (even being labeled insubordinate, fired, or some other consequence), there is no price too high to be faithful to God and what He is saying to do. This is what it means to be a spiritual leader.

You cannot lead with conviction if you're not willing and ready for it to cost. Conviction costs. If you want to cut cost, you have to cut conviction. You can have conviction or you can have complacency, and it's a willingness to endure cost that separates the two. It's why so many church leaders get into hobbies and extracurriculars to pour their passion into, because if they invested that same conviction into their calling, it would cost. (Much reduced passion in the pastorate comes from killing conviction in the heart in order to avoid cost in life.)

We need spiritual leaders with conviction and spiritual leaders of conviction. What God says is to be held in the highest regard, no matter the cost. How can you say, "I've heard from God through Scripture or by the Spirit," but when challenged and facing cost or consequence, capitulate and say, "It's okay. No big deal. It wasn't that important anyway." Is God's speaking such an insignificant thing? No, it's not! God is not a consultant. He is King. If you are not willing to get fired over what you are teaching, you have got to ask what you are teaching. If you can take it or leave it, if you can preach it or pitch it, you might be peddling something, but you are not preaching the Word of God. God's Word is a fire in the bones that can't be blown out. Conviction isn't crushed by consequence, and conviction doesn't cower in the face of cost. Conviction will pay any cost, and conviction will endure any consequence to be faithful to do what God says to do and say what God says to say.

We need to be careful about governance in the Church and structure in the Church stifling this. Talking about the right structure, the Biblical structure, is not about being unteachable. It's also not about being unaccountable. It's about being faithful. You don't want teachers getting into a place where they aren't free to teach the Word of God or pastors in a position where they are not free to lead, because someone over them is saying to go in another direction than what God says. Would you want to be operated on by a surgeon at Mayo who was being told, "Here is how we want you to do your surgery" by an oversight board of five patients who are not doctors? This needs to be corrected.

All to say, with lots of prayer and legal counsel, we pioneered a new approach to governance that fully preserves the Biblical model, while also providing accountability to pastors/elders and satisfying government requirements for churches. Should a church want help on this, please do not hesitate to reach out. We would love to help you.

As a brief overview, our Accountability Board Model is composed of both elders and volunteer congregants who serve on the board. The purpose of the Accountability Board is not to set the direction of the church or determine the approach of the church but to hold the lead pastor and other elders accountable for being faithful to the mission, the vision, and the guardrails (a list, set by the board, of all the things the lead pastor is not allowed to do). The model provides transparency and accountability, while also preserving the authority of the God-called elders of the church.

Of course, the lead pastor is evaluated and has their compensation adjusted by the volunteer board members only. So, it's important to measure what Christ considers faithful and not measure what He does not. To this end, we painstakingly went through the Scriptures to document all that God commends or corrects, and we found it thoroughly unbiblical to compensate someone based on attendance or budget size. Instead, our accountability board decided to compensate based on the faithfulness of the lead pastor and the qualitative results Christ commends.

What you measure is what will matter. Period. Stop measuring what no letter of Christ in the epistles or seven letters of Revelation ever commends or corrects and start measuring what Christ cares about. Put systems of reward and consequence in place around the right things, not the vain idol of attendance.

All to say, if your church is willing to restore Biblical governance or come under a church that has, this is highly recommended.

Appendix B

A Word to the Global Church

For our international brothers and sisters, we have a plea for you. Please do not look at the prevalence of the American Church and on account of that, seek to emulate us. You can be prevalent and impotent as much of the Church in America is today. You (and we) do not need prevalence as much as you (and we) need His power and presence.

For far too long, those around the globe have been encouraged to come to our conferences to learn how to be more successful and effective in ministry, and what they've heard, not explicitly, is the formula of our idolatry:

Excellence + Relevance – Cost =
Greatest Attendance

Man's strategies, schemes, and smarts are not the answer. The answer is what it has always been: Him! Many of you know that better than us.

Last year, we had the privilege of serving in a country that is known, generally, for being hostile to the gospel. The believers were on fire. They poured out passionate worship, freely. They prayed fervently. They cherished the Word of God and saw, and sought, the power of the Spirit in their midst. While there, I (Shane) was teaching at a pastor's conference, and I spoke on complementary, challenging, and costly Christianity. When I said, "Christianity is costly," the room erupted in shouts and celebration. I had never seen or heard a response like that before, especially on that topic. I was sure the translator made an error, so I repeated it and added, "Christianity is costly; it requires us to give all, including our lives, for the One who gave all for us." The same cheering happened again! In that moment, I wished that every single one of those men and women could come here to lead a conference and teach us how to be "successful" and "effective" in ministry.

Our prayer for you, for our brothers and sisters around the globe, is to not be swayed off course, but to stay the course, and pray that here and everywhere, there would be a first-love revolution that the Church would love God with all its heart, soul, mind, and strength.

Appendix C

Learnings about Multisite

We were surprised when God first told us that our church would have more than one location, even locations all over the world. Historically, we have been involved in helping to plant hundreds of independent churches globally and nationally, but we did not have a philosophy or desire to be a multisite church. However, when we planted Revolution Church, God gave a vision that made it clear it would be His path for us. We did not need to understand the reasons why in order to obey.

However, we can now tell you that we've observed something extremely significant. When we started our first new location, we witnessed all the grace on the house flow to that new location in record time. We (our original church body) prayed for a number of things for years before God granted them, but the second campus started experiencing them in increased measure almost immediately. On top of that, the signs and wonders He was doing here, He also did there.

We were both relieved and in awe. We were relieved, because we had wondered, with such a unique journey and all the things that God had done to forge our unique DNA over the course of our history, how that could be passed along and how we could genuinely be one body, not two. We had no idea that He would accelerate the pouring out of His grace the way that He did. We also did not know that, what He was doing in one location, He would also do in the other.

When we came to Him in prayer to both thank Him and inquire about this, we came to learn that when it's one house, the grace on the house goes to the whole, as long as there is unity with the leadership of the location pastor. That unity has to be in both the why and the how, but when that is in place, the grace flows freely. All to say, for those of you who are already multisite churches, be encouraged. The multisite model does not restrict you from pursuing a first-love revolution. Likewise, if you are contemplating going multisite, know that the DNA of a first-love revolution can travel to all of your campuses, as long as the campus pastor is unified to the vision and model.

References

Chapter Two

1. McIntosh, Gary L. "Church Movements of the Last Fifty Years in the USA." *Church Growth Network*, 13 March 2015, https://www.churchgrowthnetwork.com/freebies2/2015/3/13/church-movements-of-the-last-fifty-years-in-the-usa. Accessed 26 August 2023.

2. McIntosh, Gary L. "Church Movements of the Last Fifty Years in the USA." *Church Growth Network*, 13 March 2015, https://www.churchgrowthnetwork.com/freebies2/2015/3/13/church-movements-of-the-last-fifty-years-in-the-usa. Accessed 26 August 2023.

3. McIntosh, Gary L. "Church Movements of the Last Fifty Years in the USA." *Church Growth Network*, 13 March 2015, https://www.churchgrowthnetwork.com/freebies2/2015/3/13/church-movements-of-the-last-fifty-years-in-the-usa. Accessed 26 August 2023.

4. Barna. "Signs of Decline & Hope Among Key Metrics of Faith." *Barna.com*, 4 March 2020, https://www.barna.com/research/changing-state-of-the-church/. Accessed 27 August 2023.

5. Barna. "Signs of Decline & Hope Among Key Metrics of Faith." *Barna.com*, 4 March 2020, https://www.barna.com/research/changing-state-of-the-church/. Accessed 27 August 2023.

6. Fulks, Jeffery, et al. "State of the Bible: USA 2023." *American Bible Society*, September 2023, https://1s712.americanbible.org/state-of-the-bible/stateofthebible/State_of_the_bible-2023.pdf. Accessed 16 September 2023.

7. Jones, Jeffrey M. "U.S. Church Attendance Still Lower Than Pre-Pandemic." *Gallup News*, 26 June 2023, https://news.gallup.com/poll/507692/church-attendance-lower-pre-pandemic.aspx. Accessed 28 August 2023.

8. Barna, George. *Revolution*. Kindle ed., Tyndale, 2012, https://www.amazon.com/Revolution-George-Barna-ebook/dp/B0096VZ85G/.

9. Smith, Gregory A., et al. "In U.S., Decline of Christianity Continues at Rapid Pace." *Pew Research Center*, 17 October 2019, https://www.pewresearch.org/religion/2019/10/17/in-u-s-decline-of-christianity-continues-at-rapid-pace/. Accessed 27 August 2023.

10. McIntosh, Gary L. "Church Movements of the Last Fifty Years in the USA." *Church Growth Network*, 13 March 2015, https://www.churchgrowthnetwork. com/freebies2/2015/3/13/church-movements-of-the-last-fifty-years-in-the-usa. Accessed 26 August 2023.

11. McIntosh, Gary L. "Church Movements of the Last Fifty Years in the USA." *Church Growth Network*, 13 March 2015, https://www.churchgrowthnetwork. com/freebies2/2015/3/13/church-movements-of-the-last-fifty-years-in-the-usa. Accessed 26 August 2023.

12. The Association of Religion Data Archives, and Wen Reagan. "Church Growth Movement - Timeline Movement." *Thearda.com*, https://www.thearda.com/us-religion/history/timelines/entry?e-type=3&eid=8. Accessed 27 August 2023.

13. McIntosh, Gary L. "Church Movements of the Last Fifty Years in the USA." *Church Growth Network*, 13 March 2015, https://www.churchgrowthnetwork. com/freebies2/2015/3/13/church-movements-of-the-last-fifty-years-in-the-usa. Accessed 26 August 2023.

14. The Association of Religion Data Archives, and Wen Reagan. "Church Growth Movement - Timeline Movement." *Thearda.com*, https://www.thearda. com/us-religion/history/timelines/entry?e-type=3&eid=8. Accessed 27 August 2023.

15. Mancini, Will, and Cory Hartman. *Future Church: Seven Laws of Real Church Growth*. Kindle ed., Baker Publishing Group, 2020. https://www.amazon.com/Future-Church-Laws-Real-Growth-ebook/dp/B087RTBL71/

16. Wagner, C. Peter. *Your Church Can Grow*. Regal Books, 1976, p. 31.

17. McIntosh, Gary L. "Church Movements of the Last Fifty Years in the USA." *Church Growth Network*, 13 March 2015, https://www.churchgrowthnetwork.com/freebies2/2015/3/13/church-movements-of-the-last-fifty-years-in-the-usa. Accessed 26 August 2023.

18. The Association of Religion Data Archives, and Wen Reagan. "Church Growth Movement - Timeline Movement." *Thearda.com*, https://www.thearda.com/us-religion/history/timelines/entry?e-type=3&eid=8. Accessed 27 August 2023.

19. Outreach100. "2023 Largest Churches." Outreach 100, 2022, https://outreach100.com/largest-churches-in-america. Accessed 27 August 2023.

20. McIntosh, Gary L. "Church Movements of the Last Fifty Years in the USA." *Church Growth Network*, 13 March 2015, https://www.churchgrowthnetwork.com/freebies2/2015/3/13/church-movements-of-the-last-fifty-years-in-the-usa. Accessed 26 August 2023.

21. Kimball, Dan. *The Emerging Church: Vintage Christianity for New Generations.* Kindle ed., Zondervan, 2009. https://www.amazon.com/Emerging-Church-Dan-Kimball-ebook/dp/B000SEKK94/.

22. Kimball, Dan. *The Emerging Church: Vintage Christianity for New Generations.* Kindle ed., Zondervan, 2009. https://www.amazon.com/Emerging-Church-Dan-Kimball-ebook/dp/B000SEKK94/.

23. McIntosh, Gary L. "Church Movements of the Last Fifty Years in the USA." *Church Growth Network*, 13 March 2015, https://www.churchgrowthnetwork.com/freebies2/2015/3/13/church-movements-of-the-last-fifty-years-in-the-usa. Accessed 26 August 2023.

24. The Association of Religion Data Archives. "Missional Church Movement - Timeline Movement." *Thearda.com*, https://www.thearda.com/us-religion/history/timelines/entry?eid=24%7C3. Accessed 27 Aug 2023.

25. McIntosh, Gary L. "Church Movements of the Last Fifty Years in the USA." *Church Growth Network*, 13 March 2015, https://www.churchgrowthnetwork.com/freebies2/2015/3/13/church-movements-of-the-last-fifty-years-in-the-usa. Accessed 26 August 2023.

26. Earls, Aaron. "Where Are All the Megachurches?" *Lifeway Research*, 9 June 2017, https://research.lifeway.com/2017/06/09/where-are-all-the-megachurches/. Accessed 19 September 2023.

27. Barna, George. "American Worldview Inventory 2022 - Release #6: Only Half of Evangelical Pastors Possess a Biblical Worldview; Incidence Even Lower for Most Denominations." *Arizona Christian University*, 10 May 2022, https://www.arizonachristian.edu/wp-content/uploads/2022/05/AWVI2022_Release05_Digital.pdf. Accessed 30 August 2023.

28. Grant, Tobin. "The Great Decline: 60 years of religion in one graph." *Religion News Service*, 27 January 2014, https://religionnews.com/2014/01/27/great-decline-religion-united-states-one-graph/. Accessed 27 August 2023.

29. Smith, Gregory A. "About Three-in-Ten U.S. Adults Are Now Religiously Unaffiliated." *Pew Research Center*, 14 December 2021, https://www.pewresearch.org/religion/2021/12/14/about-three-in-ten-u-s-adults-are-now-religiously-unaffiliated/. Accessed 28 August 2023.

30. Smith, Gregory A. "About Three-in-Ten U.S. Adults Are Now Religiously Unaffiliated." *Pew Research Center*, 14 December 2021, https://www.pewresearch.org/religion/2021/12/14/about-three-in-ten-u-s-adults-are-now-religiously-unaffiliated/. Accessed 28 August 2023.

31. Nortey, Justin, and Michael Rotolo. "How COVID-19 Affected Religious Service Attendance in U.S., 2020-2022." *Pew Research Center*, 28 March 2023, https://www.pewresearch.org/religion/2023/03/28/

how-the-pandemic-has-affected-attendance-at-u-s-religious-services/. Accessed 28 August 2023.

32. Wang, Wendy. "Number 2 in 2022: The Decline in Church Attendance in COVID America." *Institute for Family Studies*, 29 December 2022, https://ifstudies.org/blog/number-2-in-2022-the-decline-in-church-attendance-in-covid-america. Accessed 28 August 2023.

33. Jones, Jeffrey M. "U.S. Church Attendance Still Lower Than Pre-Pandemic." *Gallup News*, 26 June 2023, https://news.gallup.com/poll/507692/church-attendance-lower-pre-pandemic.aspx. Accessed 28 August 2023.

34. Jones, Jeffrey M. "U.S. Church Attendance Still Lower Than Pre-Pandemic." *Gallup News*, 26 June 2023, https://news.gallup.com/poll/507692/church-attendance-lower-pre-pandemic.aspx. Accessed 28 August 2023.

35. Barna. "Pastors Share Top Reasons They've Considered Quitting Ministry in the Past Year." *Barna.com*, 27 April 2022, https://www.barna.com/research/pastors-quitting-ministry/.Accessed27August2023.

Chapter Three

1. Quinn, Dennis, et al. "The Digital Pulpit: A Nationwide Analysis of Online Sermons." *Pew Research Center*, 16 December 2019, https://www.pewresearch.org/

religion/2019/12/16/the-digital-pulpit-a-nation-wide-analysis-of-online-sermons/. Accessed 30 August 2023.

2. Quinn, Dennis, et al. "The Digital Pulpit: A Nationwide Analysis of Online Sermons." *Pew Research Center*, 16 December 2019, https://www.pewresearch.org/religion/2019/12/16/the-digital-pulpit-a-nation-wide-analysis-of-online-sermons/. Accessed 30 August 2023.

3. Quinn, Dennis. "Few U.S. sermons mention abortion, though discussion varies by religious affiliation and congregation size." *Pew Research Center*, 29 April 2020, https://www.pewresearch.org/short-reads/2020/04/29/few-u-s-sermons-mention-abortion-though-discussion-varies-by-religious-affiliation-and-congregation-size/. Accessed 30 August 2023.

4. Quinn, Dennis. "Few U.S. sermons mention abortion, though discussion varies by religious affiliation and congregation size." *Pew Research Center*, 29 April 2020, https://www.pewresearch.org/short-reads/2020/04/29/few-u-s-sermons-mention-abortion-though-discussion-varies-by-religious-affiliation-and-congregation-size/. Accessed 30 August 2023.

5. Kumar, Anugrah. "Only 37% of pastors have a Biblical worldview: Spiritual awakening 'needed in our pulpits'." *The Christian Post*, 16 May 2022, https://

www.christianpost.com/news/only-37-of-pastors-have-a-Biblical-worldview-barna.html. Accessed 30 August 2023.

6. Barna, George. "American Worldview Inventory 2022 - Release #5: Shocking Results Concerning the Worldview of Christian Pastors." *Arizona Christian University*, 10 May 2022, https://www.arizonachristian.edu/wp-content/uploads/2022/05/AWVI2022_Release05_Digital.pdf. Accessed 30 August 2023.

7. Kumar, Anugrah. "Only 37% of pastors have a Biblical worldview: Spiritual awakening 'needed in our pulpits'." *The Christian Post*, 16 May 2022, https://www.christianpost.com/news/only-37-of-pastors-have-a-Biblical-worldview-barna.html. Accessed 30 August 2023.

8. Barna, George. "American Worldview Inventory 2022 - Release #5: Shocking Results Concerning the Worldview of Christian Pastors." *Arizona Christian University*, 10 May 2022, https://www.arizonachristian.edu/wp-content/uploads/2022/05/AWVI2022_Release05_Digital.pdf. Accessed 30 August 2023.

9. Barna, George. *Revolution*. Kindle ed., Tyndale, 2012. https://www.amazon.com/Revolution-George-Barna-ebook/dp/B0096VZ85G/.

10. Barna, George. *Revolution*. Kindle ed., Tyndale, 2012. https://www.amazon.com/Revolution-George-Barna-ebook/dp/B0096VZ85G/.

11. Barna, George. *American Worldview Inventory 2021-22: The Annual Report on the State of Worldview in the United States*. Kindle ed., Arizona Christian University Press, 2022, https://www.amazon.com/American-Worldview-Inventory-2021-22-Annual/dp/1735776343/.

12. Barna, George. *American Worldview Inventory 2021-22: The Annual Report on the State of Worldview in the United States*. Kindle ed., Arizona Christian University Press, 2022, https://www.amazon.com/American-Worldview-Inventory-2021-22-Annual/dp/1735776343/.

13. Barna, George. *American Worldview Inventory 2021-22: The Annual Report on the State of Worldview in the United States*. Kindle ed., Arizona Christian University Press, 2022, https://www.amazon.com/American-Worldview-Inventory-2021-22-Annual/dp/1735776343/.

14. Barna, George. *American Worldview Inventory 2021-22: The Annual Report on the State of Worldview in the United States*. Kindle ed., Arizona Christian University Press, 2022, https://www.amazon.com/American-Worldview-Inventory-2021-22-Annual/dp/1735776343/.

15. Barna, George. *Revolution*. Kindle ed., Tyndale, 2012. https://www.amazon.com/Revolution-George-Barna-ebook/dp/B0096VZ85G/.

16. Barna, George. *American Worldview Inventory 2021-22: The Annual Report on the State of Worldview in the United States*. Kindle ed., Arizona Christian University Press, 2022, https://www.amazon.com/American-Worldview-Inventory-2021-22-Annual/dp/1735776343/.

Chapter Four

1. Barna, George. *Revolution*. Kindle ed., Tyndale, 2012. https://www.amazon.com/Revolution-George-Barna-ebook/dp/B0096VZ85G/.

2. Barna, George. *Revolution*. Kindle ed., Tyndale, 2012. https://www.amazon.com/Revolution-George-Barna-ebook/dp/B0096VZ85G/.

3. Castleman, Robbie F. "*The Last Word: The Great Commission: Ecclesiology.*" Themelios, vol. 32, no. 3, 2007, pp. 68--70, https://www.thegospelcoalition.org/themelios/article/the-last-word-the-great-commission-ecclesiology/. Accessed 18 September 2023.

Chapter Seven

1. Vaughan, Harold. "Prayerless Praying – Christ Life Ministries." *Christ Life Ministries*, 7 June 2008, https://christlifemin.org/2008/06/07/prayerless-praying/. Accessed 20 September 2023.

2. Pauley, Scott. "My Favorite Prayer Quotes." Enjoying the Journey, 2023, https://enjoyingthejourney.org/

my-favorite-prayer-quotes/. Accessed 20 September 2023.

3. Ravenhill, Leonard. *Why Revival Tarries*. Baker Publishing Group, 2004, p. 39.

Chapter Eight

1. Scharbert, Josef. "קלל." *Theological Dictionary of the Old Testament*, Translated by David E. Green, edited by Botterweck, G. Johannes, Ringgren, Helmer, and Fabry, Heinz-Josef, Eerdmans, 2004, p. 37.

2. Hill, Gary. *The Discovery Bible: New Testament*. Edited by Gary Hill and Gleason L. Archer, BMH Books, 1987. Accessed 11 October 2023.

3. Delling, Gerhard. "Λαμβάνω, Ἀναλαμβάνω, Ἀνάλημψις, Ἐπιλαμβάνω, Ἀνεπίλημπτος, Κατα-, Μεταλαμβάνω, Μετάλημψις, Παρα-, Προ-, Προσλαμβάνω, Πρόσλημψις, Ὑπολαμβάνω." *Theological Dictionary of the New Testament*, edited by Kittel, Gerhard, Bromiley, Geoffrey W., and Gerhard, Friedrich, Eerdmans, 1964–, p. 15.

4. Stauffer, Ethelbert. "Ἀγών, Ἀγωνίζομαι, Ἀντ-, Ἐπ-, Καταγωνίζομαι, Ἀγωνία." *Theological Dictionary of the New Testament* edited by Kittel, Gerhard, Bromiley, Geoffrey W., and Friedrich, Gerhard, Eerdmans, 1964–, 135.

5. Stauffer, Ethelbert. "Ἀγών, Ἀγωνίζομαι, Ἀντ-, Ἐπ-, Καταγωνίζομαι, Ἀγωνία." *Theological Dictionary of the*

New Testament edited by Kittel, Gerhard, Bromiley, Geoffrey W., and Friedrich, Gerhard, Eerdmans, 1964–, 135.

6. Barna, George K. "American Worldview Inventory 2022 Release #7: Non-Denominational Pastors Far More Likely to Hold Biblical Views than All Other D." *Arizona Christian University*, 30 August 2022, https://www.arizonachristian.edu/wp-content/uploads/2022/08/CRC_AWVIRelease_07_Digital.pdf. Accessed 31 August 2023.

Chapter Nine

1. Earth Science Australia. "WIND TOWERS." Earth Science Australia, 2021, http://earthsci.org/mineral/energy/wind_tower_iran/wind_towers.html. Accessed 18 October 2023.

2. Jackson, Bill. *The Quest for the Radical Middle: A History of the Vineyard.* Vineyard International., 2000, p. 200.

Chapter Ten

1. Barna, George K. "American Worldview Inventory 2022 Release #7: Non-Denominational Pastors Far More Likely to Hold Biblical Views than All Other D." *Arizona Christian University*, 30 August 2022, https://www.arizonachristian.edu/wp-content/uploads/2022/08/CRC_AWVIRelease_07_Digital.pdf. Accessed 31 August 2023.

2. Barna, George K. "American Worldview Inventory 2022 Release #7: Non-Denominational Pastors Far More Likely to Hold Biblical Views than All Other D." *Arizona Christian University*, 30 August 2022, https://www.arizonachristian.edu/wp-content/uploads/2022/08/CRC_AWVIRelease_07_Digital.pdf. Accessed 31 August 2023.

Chapter Twelve

1. Ravenhill, Leonard. *Why Revival Tarries*. Baker Publishing Group, 2004, p. 21.

Chapter Thirteen

1. Collins, Jim. "Concepts - BHAG." *Jim Collins*, 2023, https://www.jimcollins.com/concepts/bhag.html. Accessed 14 October 2023.

2. Barna, George. *American Worldview Inventory 2021-22: The Annual Report on the State of Worldview in the United States*. Arizona Christian University Press, 2022.

3. Hill, Gary. *The Discovery Bible: New Testament*. Edited by Gary Hill and Gleason L. Archer, BMH Books, 1987. Accessed 11 October 2023.

4. Hill, Gary. *The Discovery Bible: New Testament*. Edited by Gary Hill and Gleason L. Archer, BMH Books, 1987. Accessed 11 October 2023.

Appendix A

1. Harder, Günther. "Σπουδάζω, Σπουδή, Σπουδαῖος." *Theological Dictionary of the New Testament*, edited by Kittel, Gerhard, Bromiley, Geoffrey W., and Friedrich, Gerhard, Eerdmans, 1964–, p. 559.

Scripture References

Quoted verses are listed below. Cited verses are marked with an *.

Preface
Haggai 1:3-9

Chapter One
Luke 1:15-17
Luke 1:80
Matthew 3:2
Matthew 3:7-12

Chapter Three
Acts 20:26-27
Ezekiel 3:17-19
Ephesians 4:17-19
Matthew 16:24-25
1 Samuel 2:12-17*
Psalm 10:4
Matthew 7:16-20*

Matthew 23:15

Chapter Four
Matthew 28:18-20
Acts 1:8
1 Timothy 2:3-4*
Matthew 15:7-8
Matthew 19:16-22*
Mark 10:21
Luke 9:60
John 6:66
John 6:67
John 6:61-64
Deuteronomy 6:5
Matthew 22:37-38
Revelation 2:4
Revelation 2:2-4

Revelation 2:5
Revelation 1:20
Genesis 3:8*
Revelation 21:3
Exodus 25:8
Matthew 18:20
2 Corinthians 6:16
Ephesians 2:20-22
1 Peter 2:5
1 Corinthians 6:19*
Revelation 2:5
Matthew 22:36
Matthew 22:37-38
Matthew 28:19
Matthew 28:20*
Matthew 5:48

Chapter Five

Psalm 74:3-4
2 Corinthians 5:10
Ephesians 2:8-9*
1 Corinthians 3:10-15
Luke 12:34
Mark 12:30
Matthew 22:38
Luke 10:25-28
Ephesians 2:8-9*
1 Samuel 15:22
Romans 12:1*
Hebrews 13:15*
2 Samuel 24:24

Psalm 116:12
Psalm 20:7*
Acts 8:9-24*
Genesis 3:5
Isaiah 42:8

Chapter Six

Psalm 22:3*
Romans 12:1*
1 Samuel 2:12-17*
2 Corinthians 3:18
Revelation 12:11
2 Chronicles 13:10*
1 Peter 2:9*
Revelation 1:6*
1 Peter 2:5*
Hebrews 13:15*
Leviticus 6:12-13*
1 Thessalonians 5:17*
Psalm 141:2*
Revelation 5:8*
Revelation 8:3-4*
Exodus 30:8*
Hebrews 12:28*

Chapter Seven

Matthew 21:13
1 John 3:8*
James 5:16
Hebrews 11:6
Zephaniah 1:6

Proverbs 3:5
Habakkuk 2:14
Matthew 10:8

Chapter Eight
2 Chronicles 34:14-33*
Matthew 4:4
Genesis 12:3
Exodus 22:28
Matthew 22:40
Acts 20:26-27*
Luke 9:23*
Luke 7:47*
Luke 6:38*
2 Corinthians 9:6-13*
Genesis 14:20*
Numbers 18:21-24*
1 Peter 5:6
John 9:24
Romans 12:3
Matthew 16:24*
Galatians 2:20
Colossians 3:4
Hebrews 11:6
Philippians 2:12*
2 Timothy 3:16-17*
Matthew 7:21-23*
James 2:26
Matthew 3:8
John 6:44*
Philippians 2:13*

Matthew 5:16*
James 2:19*
Matthew 28:20*
Matthew 7:21
1 Corinthians 6:9-11*
Galatians 5:19-21*
Ephesians 5:5*
Hebrews 12:14*
Hebrews 11:6
2 Corinthians 5:7
Romans 10:17
Hebrews 11:1
Luke 18:8*
Matthew 8:10*
Mark 6:6*
Matthew 24:12
John 3:16
Revelation 2:7
Revelation 2:11
Revelation 3:5
Revelation 3:12
Matthew 10:22
John 15:6
Colossians 1:22-23
1 Corinthians 15:2
2 Timothy 2:12
Matthew 10:33
Exodus 32:1-4*
Mark 2:17*
Matthew 5:19*
Matthew 5-6*

Matthew 5:29-30*
Matthew 18:6*
Hebrews 10:29
Romans 15:7
Ephesians 1:6*
Romans 6:2*
Psalm 19:9
Acts 5:11
Acts 2:42*
Acts 2:46*
Psalm 147:11
Proverbs 14:27
Deuteronomy 10:12-13
Revelation 4:8
James 4:6-8
1 Peter 1:16
Romans 15:30
Colossians 1:29
Colossians 4:12
Romans 16*
Colossians 1:29*
John 8:44*
2 Thessalonians 2:3-7*
Romans 14:12
1 Corinthians 4:5
2 Corinthians 5:10
Ecclesiastes 12:14
Matthew 10:15
Matthew 12:36
Romans 2:16
2 Peter 3:7
Revelation 20:12

1 Corinthians 3:15*
1 Corinthians 4:7
2 Timothy 2:20-21
1 Corinthians 2:1-5*

Chapter Nine

John 14:12
1 Chronicles 28:8*
2 Chronicles 15:2*
Jeremiah 29:13*
Hebrews 11:6*
Isaiah 5:20*
Zechariah 4:6
Matthew 5:3
Ephesians 2:10*
Psalm 51:11
Psalm 105:4
Ruth 1:1
Judges 21:25*
John 6:35*
Matthew 4:4*
Isaiah 59:2
Ephesians 4:30
Acts 7:51*
1 Thessalonians 5:19*
John 1:32
Matthew 5:44
Psalm 27:8
Psalm 42:1*
Matthew 5:6
Matthew 5:8
Matthew 8:34

John 3:8
1 Thessalonians 5:19-21
Romans 12:6*
1 Thessalonians 5:21*

Chapter Ten
Luke 10:6-12
Acts 2:41
Acts 2:38-40
Acts 2:42-47*
1 Timothy 5:17-18
Galatians 2:20
Acts 8:22
1 Corinthians 3:10-15*
1 Corinthians 4:21
1 Peter 5:1-4
Exodus 20:8-11*
Acts 20:7
Acts 2:46*
Exodus 33:15
Acts 6:4
Jeremiah 3:15

Chapter Twelve
2 Chronicles 7:14*
Mark 12:30*
Matthew 28:18-20*
Matthew 16:24
Mark 12:30*

Chapter Thirteen
John 7:37-38

Acts 2:38-39
Matthew 6:14
Luke 12:31
John 15:7
Matthew 24:13
Romans 8:28
Mark 4:24
James 4:10
James 4:8
Mark 8:35
Matthew 10:41
Acts 3:19
Revelation 3:20
Matthew 6:6
James 1:25
Matthew 5:19
Luke 11:9-10
Matthew 21:21
James 1:5-6
Galatians 6:7-8
Matthew 19:29
Philippians 4:6-7
Jeremiah 29:13
Luke 17:9-10
Hebrews 11:6
Acts 2:13
Luke 19:17
John 5:44
2 Chronicles 16:9*
Hebrews 11:6*
Jeremiah 18:7-10
Deuteronomy 32:16*

Genesis 6:6*
Ephesians 4:30*
Psalm 2:4*
Matthew 20:34*
1 Kings 14:22*
Psalm 24:3-4*
Psalm 15*
Matthew 18:20*
Psalm 22:3*
Matthew 7:13-14
1 Corinthians 14:25
Romans 5:10*
Colossians 1:21*
Hebrews 11:1
Hebrews 11:6
Matthew 8:10
Luke 18:8
Luke 2:37
1 Samuel 13:14
1 Corinthians 9:22
Galatians 2:20
John 14:15*
John 15:10-11*
Matthew 11:30
Matthew 23:4*
2 Corinthians 4:17*
Matthew 19:22*
John 14:15*
Numbers 12:3*
John 12:49*
John 5:19*
Isaiah 55:8

Ecclesiastes 3:1
Colossians 3:23-24*
2 Corinthians 11:22-28*
1 Corinthians 7:32-35*
Matthew 6:19-21*
Matthew 10:42*
Mark 10:29*
1 John 1:8
Psalm 139:23-24
Isaiah 6:5*
2 Timothy 3:16-17
2 Peter 1:2-3
Acts 14:14*
Romans 16:17*
2 Corinthians 8:23*
Philippians 2:25*
1 Corinthians 4:6-10*
1 Corinthians 12:28*
Ephesians 4:11-12

Chapter Fourteen
Matthew 7:26
Matthew 25:3
Matthew 7:27
Matthew 25:10-13
Matthew 7:26
Isaiah 61:3*
Psalm 1:3*

Chapter Fifteen
Acts 11:29-30*
1 Peter 5:1-2*

Titus 1:5,7*
1 Timothy 5:17*
Romans 12:8*
1 Timothy 3:2*

Titus 1:9*
1 Timothy 5:17*
Acts 4:19-20

Made in United States
North Haven, CT
19 May 2024